DISCOVER BEIJING

THE CITY'S HISTORY & CULTURE REDEFINED

Hong Zhu and Li Yangquan

Picture Credits
Authors: 13, 17, 18–19, 21, 22–23, 28–29, 30–31, 33, 38–39, 49, 50–51, 52, 53–54, 59, 64–65, 68–69, 74–75, 76–77, 78, 79, 80–81, 86–87, 88, 92–93, 106, 110–111, 112, 116–117, 119, 121, 122, 133, 134–135, 136–137, 141, 146–147, 148, 165.
Quanjing: 10–11, 15, 16, 24–25, 26, 41, 42–43, 46–47, 48, 55, 61, 63, 67, 73, 82, 84–85, 90–91, 96–97, 98, 99, 100–101, 102–103, 105, 109, 115, 123, 124–125, 126–127, 130–131, 132, 138–139, 142–143, 144–145, 149, 150, 152–153, 154–155, 157, 158–159, 161, 162, 166–167, 168–169, 170–171, 172–173.
Wang Miao: 44–45, 56–57, 71, 95, 164.
Lee Yin Peng: 35–36

© 2007 Marshall Cavendish International (Asia) Private Limited

Published by Marshall Cavendish Editions
An imprint of Marshall Cavendish International
1 New Industrial Road, Singapore 536196

All rights reserved

No part of this publication may be reproduced, stored in a retrieval system or transmitted, in any form or by any means, electronic, mechanical, photocopying, recording or otherwise, without the prior permission of the copyright owner. Request for permission should be addressed to the Publisher, Marshall Cavendish International (Asia) Private Limited, 1 New Industrial Road, Singapore 536196. Tel: (65) 6213 9300, fax: (65) 6285 4871. E-mail: genref@sg.marshallcavendish.com. Online bookstore: www.marshallcavendish.com/genref.

This publication represents the opinions and views of the author based on her personal experience, knowledge and research. The information in this book serves as a general guide only. The reader is advised to consult a medical doctor, clinical nutritionist or professional trainer before starting any form of treatment or exercise. The author and publisher have used their best efforts in preparing this book and disclaim liability rising directly and indirectly from the use and application of this book.

Other Marshall Cavendish Offices:
Marshall Cavendish Ltd. 119 Wardour Street, London W1F 0UW, UK • Marshall Cavendish Corporation. 99 White Plains Road, Tarrytown NY 10591-9001, USA • Marshall Cavendish International (Thailand) Co Ltd. 253 Asoke, 12th Flr, Sukhumvit 21 Road, Klongtoey Nua, Wattana, Bangkok 10110, Thailand • Marshall Cavendish (Malaysia) Sdn Bhd, Times Subang, Lot 46, Subang Hi-Tech Industrial Park, Batu Tiga, 40000 Shah Alam, Selangor Darul Ehsan, Malaysia

Marshall Cavendish is a trademark of Times Publishing Limited

National Library Board Singapore Cataloguing in Publication Data

Hong, Zhu, 1967-
Discover Beijing: The city's history and culture redefined / Hong Zhu and Li Yangquan. – Singapore : Marshall Cavendish Editions, c2007.
p. cm.

ISBN-13 : 978-981-261-364-6
ISBN-10 : 981-261-364-1

1. Historic sites – China – Beijing. 2. Beijing (China) – Social life and customs. 3. Beijing (China) – Guidebooks. I. Li, Yangquan.
II. Title.

DS795.A5
951.156 -- dc22   SLS2007004746

Printed in China

CONTENTS

Preface	8
Ancient Bridges	10
Archways	13
Baiyunguan (White Clouds Taoist Temple)	14
Beijing Concert Hall	17
Central Business District	18
Chang'an Avenue	21
Changdian Temple Fair	24
Chaoyang Park	27
City Gates and Walls of Beijing	30
Courtyard Houses (Siheyuan)	33
Dashazi Art District	35
Dazhalan	37
Diaoyutai	39
Ditan (The Altar of the Earth)	41
Dongjiaomin Lane	44
Fangshan Restaurant	46
Fayuan Temple	49
Finance Street	50
Former Execution Ground	52
Former Interim Government Office of Duan Qirui	53
Former Residence of Cao Xueqin	55
Former Residence of Prince Gong	57
Former Residence of Song Qingling	59
Grand View Garden (Daguanyuan)	61
Guozijian (The Imperial College)	62
Huangchenggen	64
Hutong	66
Jinghang Grand Canal	70
Jing Shan Park (Scenery Hill)	72
Kunming Lake	75
Liulichang	77
Long Corridor	79
Longfu Temple	80
Man-Han Banquet	82
Ming Tombs	83
Museums of Beijing	86

National Grand Theatre	88
Pagoda	89
Panjiayuan Market	92
Peking Opera	94
Peking Roast Duck	96
Peking University	98
Qianmen	100
Qianmen Railway Station	102
Qipao	104
Sanlitun	107
Shejitan (Zhongshan Park)	108
Shichahai	110
Snacks	113
Taimiao (Cultural Palace of the Working People)	116
Taoranting Park	119
Teahouses	120
The Bell and Drum Towers (Zhonggulou)	123
The Forbidden City	126
The Great Wall	130
The Imperial Archive	133
The Olympic Village	134
The Temple of the Reclining Buddha (Wofosi)	136
Tian'anmen Square	138
Tiantan (The Altar of Heaven)	142
Time-Honoured Brands	146
Tsinghua University	149
Wangfujing	151
Yiheyuan (Summer Palace)	156
Yonghegong Lama Temple	161
Yuandadu (Yuan Capital Relics Park)	163
Yuanmingyuan (Old Summer Palace of the Qing Dynasty)	165
Yunju Temple	171
Zhongnanhai	172
Chronology of China's Dynasties	174
Map of China	175
Map of Beijing	176

SUBJECT INDEX

 Ancient Architecture

Ancient Bridges 10
Archways 13
City Gates and Walls of Beijing 30
Courtyard Houses (Siheyuan) 33
Dazhalan 37
Ditan (The Altar of the Earth) 41
Former Interim Government Office of Duan Qirui 55
Former Residence of Prince Gong 57
Former Residence of Song Qingling 59
Guozijian (The Imperial College) 62
Huangchenggen 64
Hutong 66
Long Corridor 79
Ming Tombs 83
Pagoda 89
Qianmen 100
Qianmen Railway Station 102
The Bell and Drum Towers (Zhonggulou) 123
The Forbidden City 126
The Great Wall 130
The Imperial Archive 133
Tiantan (The Altar of Heaven) 142

 Places of Worship

Baiyunguan (White Clouds Taoist Temple) 14
Fayuan Temple 49
The Temple of the Reclining Buddha (Wofosi) 136
Yonghegong Lama Temple 161
Yunju Temple 171

 Parks

Chaoyang Park 27
Ditan (The Altar of the Earth) 41
Grand View Garden (Daguanyuan) 61
Jing Shan Park (Scenery Hill) 72
Kunming Lake 75
Long Corridor 79
Shejitan (Zhongshan Park) 108
Shichahai 110
Taimiao (Cultural Palace of Working People) 116
Taoranting Park 119
Tiantan (The Altar of Heaven) 142
Yiheyuan (Summer Palace) 156

 Commercial Areas

Central Business District 18
Chang'an Avenue 21
Finance Street 50
Longfu Temple 80
Qianmen Railway Station 103
Sanlitun 107
Shichahai 110
Wangfujing 151

Historical Interest

Ancient Bridges 10
City Gates and Walls of Beijing 30
Dongjiaomin Lane 44
Fangshan Restaurant 46
Former Execution Ground 52
Former Interim Government Office of Duan Qirui 53
Former Residence of Prince Gong 57
Former Residence of Song Qingling 59
Jinghang Grand Canal 70
Jing Shan Park (Scenery Hill) 72
Kunming Lake 75
Liulichang 77
Longfu Temple 80
Man-Han Banquet 82
Museums of Beijing 86
Peking Opera 94
Peking University 98
Qipao 104
Tian'anmen Square 138
Time-Honoured Brands 146
Tsinghua University 149
Wangfujing 151
Yiheyuan (Summer Palace) 156
Yuandadu (Yuan Capital Relics Park) 163
Yuanmingyuan (Old Summer Palace of the Qing Dynasty) 165

 Restricted Area

Diaoyutai 39
Former Interim Government Office of Duan Qirui 55
Zhongnanhai 172

 Cultural Interest

Beijing Concert Hall 17
Changdian Temple Fair 24
Dashanzi Art District 35
Former Residence of Cao Xueqin 55
Grand View Garden (Daguanyuan) 61
Liulichang 77
National Grand Theatre 88
Peking Opera 94
Qipao 104
Teahouses 120

 Lifestyle

Changdian Temple Fair 24
Dazhalan 37
Fangshan Restaurant 46
Man-Han Banquet 82
Panjiayuan Market 92
Peking Opera 94
Peking Roast Duck 96
Peking University 98
Qipao 104
Shejitan (Zhongshan Park) 108
Shichahai 110
Snacks 113
Teahouses 120
The Olympic Village 134
Time-Honoured Brands 146
Tsinghua University 149

PREFACE

We have lived in Beijing for a number of years. Only after all these years do we begin to have a better understanding of the city and gradually become a part of it. The laid-back attitude typical of the people of this city frequently gives us a sense of nostalgia.

Beijing was once a city of emperors, generals and ministers. Although other cities such as Xi'an, Luoyang, Kaifeng and Nanjing were once capitals of China, the historical changes in Beijing are the most recent. It was only a hundred years ago that Beijing was the city of emperors and generals and their influence can still be felt in this city.

At the same time, Beijing is for the common people. In the first half of the 20th century, famous Chinese writers such as Lin Yutang, Liang Shiqiu and Zhou Zuoren took up residence in Beijing. Among them was Lao She, who wrote many novels based on the lives of the common people of Beijing.

Visitors know Beijing for its ancient architecture and scenic spots. However, for the historical events that took place in this city and the complexity of the changes, it may take a lifetime for one to fully appreciate it.

Beijing is now a city of rapid changes and modernisation. Places that are rich in historical flavour are slowly losing their original splendour. At the same time, modernisation is giving the city a new energy and making it seem younger than it really is.

We have drawn a new map for Beijing. This book is about new impressions of Beijing based on its old city charms. The old Beijing city may not be found now, but its influence on the present city will go on for a long time to come.

The Authors
January, 2007

DISCOVER BEIJING

DISCOVER BEIJING | 11

  ANCIENT **BRIDGES**

There are not many bridges and rivers in Beijing, but they all have a significant place in its history.

Jinshui (Golden Water) Bridge in front of Tian'anmen gate is probably the "noblest" bridge in China as it was meant only for the imperial family's use. During the Ming and Qing dynasties, when emperors took up residence in the Forbidden City,

The Shiqikong Bridge at Yiheyuan.

this bridge was strictly off-limits to the commoners. Jinshui Bridge actually comprises five separate white marble bridges. The one in the middle—known as Yu Lu Bridge (Imperial Road Bridge)—is wider than the other four and was meant exclusively for the emperor's use. The foot of the bridge is decorated with four stone lions and two ornamental columns, which are regarded as auspicious symbols by the Chinese people.

In 1924, the last emperor of China, Puyi, abdicated and was banished from Beijing. Following this, Jinshui Bridge was open to the public and for the first time the common folks were allowed on it. Today, Jinshui Bridge is a popular spot where tourists take photographs. At sunrise and at dusk, the national guards march across Jinshui Bridge to Tian'anmen Square for the flag-raising and lowering ceremonies, which always draw a massive crowd.

Another ancient bridge in Beijing that is worth mentioning once captured Marco Polo's heart. He found the bridge so exquisitely constructed that he felt no other bridges in the world could match up to it. Known to the West as the "Marco Polo Bridge", Lugou Bridge was built in 1189 during the Jin Dynasty and is located about 15 metres southwest of Beijing city. It measures 266.5 metres in length and is made of white marble. Spanning across Lugou River, it is lined with two rows of balustrades topped with posts graced by figures of lions—one of the key attractions of the bridge.

Lugou Bridge will always remind the Chinese people of the Second Sino-Japanese War. This was the scene of a clash between Japanese and Chinese forces on 7 July 1937 that sparked off an all-out offensive by the Japanese across northern China.

Other ancient bridges that can be found in Beijing include Beihai Bridge in Beihai Park, Yudai Bridge and Shiqikong Bridge in the Summer Palace (Yiheyuan) and Wugong Bridge of Zhongnanhai.

ARCHWAYS

A typical archway that can be seen in the city of Beijing.

Old Beijing was famous for its archways (*pai lou*). An archway was like the main gate of a group of buildings or a street, but it was primarily decorative. There used to be an archway on every major street and road in old Beijing—57 of them reportedly. They were usually built to commemorate prominent intellectual personalities or government officials for their contributions to society and were representative of the unique architectural styles of the buildings in the streets.

The archway usually comprised four columns—forming three arches—making up a wide main gate in the centre and a smaller gate on each side. The sturdy archways were decorated with intricate designs and some of them lasted for hundreds of years.

Many archways in Beijing have been demolished. They include the archways at both ends of Chang'an Avenue and the one in front of Zhengyangmen Street. The archways were removed when the roads were widened as the city modernised. Several archways have been preserved and they can be found at the entrances of temples, like the one at the entrance of Yonghegong Temple. Other archways that can be found in Beijing include the ones at the entrances of the Summer Palace (Yiheyuan), the Imperial College (Guozijian), Dazhalan and Shichahai's Lotus Market.

> **LOCATION:**
>
> Guozijian Jie, Dong Cheng District, is the only street on which a few memorial archways can be seen.
>
> You can get there by subway, getting off at Yonghegong station.

BAIYUNGUAN
(White Clouds Taoist Temple)

Baiyunguan (White Clouds Taoist Temple) is the largest Taoist temple in Beijing. It was called Tianchang Temple during the Tang Dynasty and Taiji Temple during the Jin Dynasty (1115–1234). During the Yuan Dynasty, it was renamed Changchun Temple after the famous Taoist master of the time—Qiu Chuji, founder of the Dragon Gate Sect of Taoism—whose Taoist name was Changchun.

In 1221, at the invitation of Genghis Khan, Qiu Chuji, who was then in his 70s, embarked on a long journey into Mongolia to meet with the Mongol leader. His journey took him across today's Inner Mongolia, Xinjiang and Central Asia and is depicted in the book *Record of a Journey to the West* by Li Zhichang, a disciple of Qiu who accompanied him on his journey.

The key objective for Qiu's meeting with Genghis Khan was to advise him against resorting to violence in his conquest of China. Qiu also pointed out that the governing of a nation should be founded on respect for heaven and a love for the people.

Genghis Khan showed great respect to Qiu as a Taoist master and heeded his teachings, which helped in preventing a huge loss of innocent lives when the Mongolian troops headed south and crushed the Jin Dynasty. Subsequently, Genghis Khan put Qiu in charge of Taoist affairs throughout the country and renamed Tianchang Temple as Changchun Temple.

Upon his return to Beijing in 1224, Qiu Chuji took up residence in Changchun Temple till his death in 1227. Changchun Temple was renamed Baiyunguan—its present name—in the Ming Dynasty.

Baiyunguan is now known for its temple fair, which is held annually during the Spring Festival. The temple also commemorates Qiu Chuji's birthday, which falls on the 19th day of the 1st lunar month. This day is known as Yanjiu Festival. The temple is still popular among Taoists, mainly because Qiu Chuji—the great sage of Taoism—had once been a resident there.

Baiyunguan is filled with devotees on Taoist festivals.

LOCATION:
6 Baiyunguan Jie, Xibianmenwai, Xuanwu District.

16　DISCOVER BEIJING

Temple fair at Baiyunguan during the Spring Festival.

BEIJING **CONCERT HALL**

Beijing Concert Hall is located at Liubukou along West Chang'an Boulevard. Built in 1927 to house a cinema, the building was converted into a concert hall in 1960. Elegant and dignified in its black and white marble structure, it is the first modern concert hall in China.

After it was almost completely destroyed during the Cultural Revolution (1966–1976) as "an icon of Rightist Bourgeois-Revisionism", Beijing Concert Hall was closed for renovation in 1979 and reopened in 1986. Today, it has a seating capacity of 1,024. With a modern architectural design, the present-day Beijing Concert Hall boasts a much better acoustic quality, attracting well-known international performers.

Beijing Concert Hall's resident orchestra is the Central Philharmonic Society of China. Other than providing an excellent venue for world-class music performances, Beijing Concert Hall is also popular among music lovers for the lectures and exhibitions that are held there.

LOCATION:
1 Beixinhua Jie, Xicheng District.
You can get there by subway, getting off at Xidan station.

Beijing Concert Hall at Liubukou.

18   DISCOVER BEIJING

DISCOVER BEIJING   19

CENTRAL BUSINESS DISTRICT

World Trade Centre—the epicentre of Beijing's CBD.

Beijing's Central Business District (CBD) is located in the eastern part of the city. Its development can be traced back to the 1990s. It is an area that centres around Jianguomenwai Avenue and Chaoyangmenwai Street and occupies an area of about 10 square kilometres between the East 2nd Ring Road and the East 3rd Ring Road.

This area was chosen as Beijing's CBD not only because it boasts good infrastructure and is a vibrant business hub popular with foreigners, but it is also the site of foreign embassies in Beijing.

With the World Trade Centre building as the epicentre for this new commercial area, many high-rise commercial buildings have been built, such as Motorola Plaza, Kerry Centre, Hewlett Packard Plaza and Jianwai SOHO. Within its vicinity, there are also many hotels, residential buildings and entertainment venues. More than half of the city's tallest commercial buildings and hotels are located in this area and three of Beijing's tallest skyscrapers are found here.

Beijing's CBD has attracted many multinational companies, foreign-funded banks and other commercial firms to set up offices here. Some of the multinational companies that have their offices located in the CBD include Samsung, Dell, Hong Kong and Shanghai Bank and Citibank.

LOCATION:
World Trade Centre 1 Jianguomenwai Dajie.
You can get there by subway, getting off at Guomao station.

CHANG'AN AVENUE

Chang'an Avenue is one of the busiest roads and sees massive traffic jams every evening.

Chang'an Avenue is the most famous street in Beijing. It runs across the most important political, economic and cultural areas in the city. It also connects the two busiest commercial areas—Wangfujing and Xidan.

The main stretch of Chang'an Avenue begins from Gongzhufen Intersection at the West 3rd Ring Road to Guomao Intersection at the East 3rd Ring Road. This part of the street is about 14 kilometres long and it is here that many of the political, administrative, cultural, financial and commercial institutions are located. Chang'an Avenue runs parallel to Tian'anmen Square and the Forbidden City, which are located in the heart of Beijing.

Renovation work goes on regularly along Chang'an Avenue. Foreigners are often puzzled as to why the Beijing government puts so much effort in renovating and beautifying Chang'an Avenue. To understand this, one must first understand the idea of "*mian zi*".

Mian zi means "face" or "face value" in Chinese. For a Chinese, appearances are important. In order not to "lose face", a Chinese would try to present his best possessions before others, even if it means he has to pretend to be someone he is not.

The same rule applies to the Beijing government. When visitors see Chang'an Avenue, they would get the impression that the rest of Beijing is as modern and developed as this street. Hence Chang'an Avenue can be regarded as the "face" of Beijing.

22　DISCOVER BEIJING

The spectacular sight of Chang'an Avenue at night.

DISCOVER BEIJING 23

CHANGDIAN TEMPLE FAIR

The fair started as a small lantern fair during the Ming Dynasty in 1520. During the Qing Dynasty, it became known as a fair for books and antiques. When the Qing government was overthrown in 1912, business at the fair was affected by the political upheaval and went into decline. After the People's Republic of China was

DISCOVER BEIJING

Changdian Temple Fair is as popular today as it was during the Ming and Qing dynasties.

established in 1949, the fair enjoyed a period of revival before it was banned for 37 years at the beginning of the Cultural Revolution (1966–1976). The present Beijing government is making plans to bring back its glory days.

Changdian was originally a small lane outside the southern gate of Beijing during the Yuan Dynasty. Several workshops that manufactured tiles were set up there to supply glazed tiles for palaces. Hence, it used to be known also as Liulichang (Glazed Tiles Workshop) Changdian.

Changdian temple fair was the largest of eight annual temple fairs in Beijing at that time. It was also the longest in duration—running for 16 days beginning from the 1st day of the 1st lunar month. In 1918, Changdian temple fair became the only temple fair in Beijing that was sponsored by the government.

Changdian temple fair was also famous for snacks, handicrafts and toys. Vendors sold goldfish, firecrackers, slings, lanterns and kites. Toys for children ranged from large colourful pinwheels and clay figurines to wax figurines of ducks that could be set afloat on water. Rarely did a visitor leave the temple fair empty-handed.

In the olden days, when there were no supermarkets and department stores, the temple fairs were the only places where toys could be bought. If a child did not buy the toy he fancied, he had to wait for the next temple fair.

The Changdian temple fair was revived in recent years. Instead of its original 16 days, it now runs for six days during the Spring Festival. Today's Changdian temple fair is more like a bazaar or flea market where visitors can get a good bargain for books, music CDs, paintings, handicrafts and toys. Visitors are also treated to performances such as traditional marriage rituals and folk dances.

Chui tang ren—the Candy Blower—keeping alive a traditional folk art.

LOCATION:

From the crossing of Hepingmen to the crossing to Hufangqiao, Xuanwu District.

You can get there by subway, getting off at Hepingmen station.

CHAOYANG PARK

Chaoyang Park, situated near the East 4th Ring Road, was built in 1984 and it was first called Shuiduizi Park. Back then, Chaoyang District was still a suburb of Beijing and was not as populated as it is now. With the modernisation and expansion of Beijing city, it has now become the business district of the city.

Chaoyang Park has been redesigned and there are plans to make it the biggest city park in Asia—with a land area of 713 acres, from Liangmaqiao Road to the north, Chaoyang Park Road to the west, the East 4th Ring Road to the east and South Chaoyang Park Road to the south.

With the new Chaoyang Park, people in the eastern part of Beijing would have a more interesting place for leisure and relaxation in the bustling city. They can take a stroll or exercise in this big, beautiful, landscaped city park. In recent years, more scenic spots have been added within the park and a total of 412 acres of trees and lawn have been planted.

Many sporting events that were once held at Beijing Stadium and Workers Stadium are now being held at Chaoyang Park. In the 2008 Beijing Olympic Games, the beach volleyball games will be held in Chaoyang Park.

Chaoyang Park is a place for visitors of all ages. The sparkling green lake in the park is especially delightful. There, visitors can row boats and take in the beautiful scenery.

To the south and west gates of Chaoyang Park are bars and restaurants serving a wide variety of local and international cuisines. With this new location for dining and entertainment, Chaoyang Park is not only the "lung" of Beijing—as many locals refer to it as—but also its "stomach". It is unquestionably a great place worth visiting.

LOCATION:
1 Chaoyanggongyuan Nanlu, Chaoyang District.

DISCOVER BEIJING   29

One of the annual carnivals held at Chaoyang Park.

CITY GATES AND WALLS OF BEIJING

The inner city of Beijing had nine city gates built into the city walls that were once vital to its defence. The oldest city walls of Beijing were built during the Jin Dynasty (1115–1234). The city of Beijing was modelled on the layout of Bianliang City—the capital city of the Song Dynasty—and it took 1,200,000 people and three years to expand it and have the walls constructed.

The perimeter of the city wall at the time was 18 kilometres. Unfortunately, the wall was destroyed when the Mongolians

Tian'anmen Gate is one of the most visited city gates in Beijing.

invaded Beijing. As the new rulers of China, the Mongolians then built a new capital city to the north of the former Beijing city. It was called Yuandadu (Yuan Capital) at the time and its city wall measured 30 kilometres in perimeter. Parts of the walls built by the Mongolians can still be seen at today's Yuan Capital Relics Park in Beijing.

After the collapse of the Yuan Dynasty, a new city was constructed during the early years of the Ming Dynasty. This time, the size of Beijing city was further expanded. In the middle of the Ming Dynasty, an outer city was also constructed. However, only the southern half of the outer city was built as the government ran out of funds.

The walls built during the Jin and Yuan dynasties were of clay. The Mongolians also built enceintes (enclosure gates for defence) outside the main city gates. At these enceintes were towers where archers were stationed. Qianmen (Qian Gate) was originally the enceinte of Zhengyangmen (Zhengyang Gate).

In the Ming Dynasty, bricks were added to the clay walls to make them sturdier. In the Qing Dynasty, a part of the city wall beside Zuo'anmen (Zuo'an Gate) was taken down to make way for a railway that connected Beijing to Tianjin. Following that, people started removing parts of the city walls and using them as materials for their buildings.

After the founding of the People's Republic of China in 1949, many local architects suggested that the ancient city of Beijing be conserved as part of China's heritage, but their suggestions were rejected. The city walls of Beijing were gradually dismantled as the city modernised.

Today, only parts of the city walls can still be seen in Beijing. They include the walls surrounding the Forbidden City, Tian'anmen (Tian'an Gate), Zhengyangmen (Zhengyang Gate) and Deshengmen (Desheng Gate).

In 1998, the city government of Beijing spent one million yuan to restore a 200-metre city wall of Xibianmen (Xibian Gate). It is the last remaining wall that dates back to the Ming Dynasty. Now it is a popular tourist spot.

LOCATION:

Deshengmen: Dengshengmen Jianlou, Bei'erhuan Lu, Xicheng District.

Qianmen: Qianmen Gate, Chongwen District, South end of Tian'anmen Square.

COURTYARD HOUSES (Siheyuan)

A typical courtyard house in Beijing.

Courtyard houses (Siheyuan) are a signature of Beijing. Actually, the basic structure of a courtyard house developed during the Western Zhou Dynasty. Somehow, courtyard houses have ended up becoming a representative form of Beijing's residential houses. The courtyard houses that can be found in Beijing today date back to the Ming and Qing dynasties.

A courtyard house is shaped like a box. In the past, people in Beijing fancied living in a house that had its own private entrance and compound. It was considered ideal to have several generations living together in a courtyard house.

A courtyard house comprises an outer courtyard and an inner courtyard. The outer courtyard is composed of the servants' rooms, the living room and the guestrooms. The inner courtyard is composed of the principal room (*zheng fang*), the side room (*xiang fang*) and the wing room (*er fang*). In bigger courtyard houses, one will see several inner courtyards within the compound. Although they are all called courtyard houses, their sizes vary in accordance with the wealth of their owners. A rich family's courtyard house would certainly look more sophisticated and luxurious.

A courtyard house that is composed of several courtyard compounds is known as a *da zhai men*, or courtyard mansion. Most of these mansions used to belong to the imperial families or court officials.

In front of the gate of a courtyard mansion belonging to an imperial official, there would usually be a stone on which a person could step to get on a horse or a sedan chair. These stones were in the shape of cubes or drums and were carved with elaborate patterns.

Courtyard mansions usually had sheltered corridors for easy access within the property during bad weather. Private gardens in the back were usually beautifully landscaped with miniature hills and ponds.

Other features of courtyard houses include the front gate, door stones (*men dun*), screen walls (*ying bi*) and screen doors (*chui hua men* or *ping men*). The screen door refers to a special gate inside the courtyard house and is carved with patterns of flowers. It separates the living quarter and the bedrooms.

There is no central heating system in the courtyard house. One has to light a stove using honeycomb briquette, so it is much colder living in a courtyard house than in a modern apartment in winter.

Visitors to Beijing who are interested in viewing a courtyard mansion can visit one of the former princes' mansions that are now used as restaurants or museums.

Several hotels in Beijing operate out of courtyard houses, such as Wofosi Hotel at the foot of Fragrant Hills (Xiang Shan). The guestrooms are furnished with wooden beds, rattan chairs and wooden furniture in the Ming and Qing styles.

DASHANZI ART DISTRICT

The people's love for Chairman Mao is reflected in this art gallery in Dashanzi Art District.

Popularly known as 798 Art District, the Dashanzi Art District is located at Jiuxianqiao Road in the Chaoyang District. Dashanzi started gaining popularity as an art hub in early 2000 when local Chinese artists and art groups set up their studios in this compound of disused factories and warehouses.

Formerly known as 798 Factory, these state-owned factories and old warehouses were constructed in the late 1950s when the Chinese government was steering the country towards industrialisation with an emphasis on heavy industry. The Bauhaus-style factory buildings were designed by East German architects and funded by the former Soviet Union.

Abandoned by the government in the 1990s, these factories, which have amazingly high ceilings and natural light, were first noticed by officials from the Central Academy of Fine Arts in search of inexpensive factory space for its sculpture department. Soon they were joined by independent local artists who also took advantage of the inexpensive factory space to set up their studios.

LOCATION:
Jiuxianqiao Road. South of Dashanzi Bridge Chaoyang District.

Currently, about 100,000 square metres of factory space in this compound are rented out to local and international art galleries, studios, book stores, cafés and restaurants. The occupants include reputed contemporary art galleries such as 798 Space, Beijing-Tokyo Art Project, Tang Contemporary Art, 798 Photo Gallery, 798/Red Gate Gallery and Chen Xin Dong International Contemporary Art.

The galleries in Dashanzi Art District have exhibited works by established Chinese artists such as Zhang Xiaogang and Fang Lijun, as well as by foreign artists from Europe, the USA, Australia and Asia. These galleries are also frequented by art buyers from all over the world. The art district also plays host to a number of regular art festivals such as the Beijing Biennale and Dashanzi International Art Festival.

Today's revolution in art—a reminiscence of the 50's industrial revolution?

DAZHALAN

Dazhalan is a popular market street in Beijing. Dazhalan literally means "big wooden gate" in Chinese. The locals call it "Dashilanr", though it should be pronounced as "Dazhalan". This pronunciation is a reminiscence of the old spoken Chinese that is still widely used in Beijing today.

In 1644, after the capital of the Qing Dynasty was established in the city of Beijing, the Manchurians took up a series of initiatives to suppress the Han Chinese and other minority races. In addition to political suppression, the Manchurians seized the properties of the Han Chinese. This sparked several revolts from the people of Beijing. In order to stabilise the situation, the Qing government undertook a number of measures, such as suspending tax collection, to relieve the crisis.

The Qing government also tightened security within the city by stationing additional troops, increasing the number of patrols and enforcing a stringent system to monitor the movement of people at the city gates. Big wooden gates were also erected at the ends of streets and lanes outside the inner city of Beijing. At night, these gates would be closed and curfews were imposed.

Usually, the shops in a street would fully finance the building of the big wooden gates. The most famous wooden gate was built outside Qianmen (Qian Gate). The famous Langfangsitiao Lane near Qianmen—with its many big stores that date back for 200 to 300 years—was owned by rich businessmen. In order to safeguard their properties, the businessmen built two large, elaborately designed wooden gates. Gradually, Langfangsitiao Lane became popular because of these big wooden gates and was then called "Dazhalan" by the people of Beijing.

In the Qing Dynasty, Dazhalan measured 275 metres long and 5 metres wide. There were about 80 stores, restaurants and theatres at that time. They included many popular stores that were time-honoured brands. For instance, Liubiju, a pickles store, was founded as early as the Ming Dynasty. Tongrentang, a traditional Chinese medicine store, has a history of more than 200 years. These stores usually put up big signboards to draw attention. At night, the signboards were adorned with dozens of lit lanterns to draw customers.

The 15th day of the 1st lunar month is the Lantern Festival

Dazhalan, or—as the locals fondly call it—Dashilanr.

LOCATION:

Around Qianmenwai.

You can go there by subway, getting off at Qianmen station.

in China and it was a tradition for people in Beijing to visit Dazhalan. Every store in Dazhalan hung up big, brightly-lit lanterns and the street swarmed with people. The lanterns in Dazhalan were probably the most impressive in Beijing. Every year, new designs were featured and artisans came up with a variety of new lanterns to delight the visitors.

Traditionally, stores in Dazhalan did not advertise their products and services. They strongly believed that everyone in Beijing—and even all across China—was familiar with their brands. Therefore, there was no need for advertisements. This tradition lasted for a long time until recently, with the increasing number of Western brands finding their way into the hearts of the people, these time-honoured brands have started to advertise in newspapers and on TV as well.

DIAOYUTAI

Diaoyutai ('fishing terrace' in English) is located to the west of Sanlihe Road. It was the compound of an imperial mansion that was first constructed in the Jin Dynasty (1115–1234) and got its name when a court official named Wang Yu—disguised as a fisherman—lived in seclusion there.

Its main lake Yuyuantan (Yuyuan Lake) has its sources in the natural springs at the bottom of the lake and spring water from West Hill (Xi Shan). Together with Taiyehu (Taiye Lake), which was also built at about the same time, they were water parks meant exclusively for the use of the imperial families of the Jin Dynasty for leisure activities such as boating and fishing.

Emperor Aizong of the Jin Dynasty once compared Diaoyutai with the famous Jintai—also an angling terrace—constructed by King Zhao (311–279 B.C.) of the kingdom of Yan. King Zhao once placed a pile of gold on the terrace and promised to give it to any wise men who were willing to serve him. His strategy worked and with the assistance of these talented people, King Zhao soon created a powerful kingdom and defeated his bitter enemy, the Kingdom of Qi. Once again, Jintai was piled with gold and other treasures, all of which were plundered from the Kingdom of Qi.

When Beijing was besieged by the Mongolians, Emperor Aizong committed suicide upon his defeat. In the Yuan Dynasty,

A night's stay at the Diaoyutai State Guesthouse can be an extravagant experience for most people.

Diaoyutai was converted into a private villa by a rich and powerful official of the time and it was renamed "Wang Liu Tang" (Hall of Ten Thousand Willow Trees).

During the reign of Emperor Qianlong of the Qing Dynasty, Diaoyutai once again became a recreation venue for the imperial family. Yuyuan Lake was expanded and the terraces were rebuilt. Instead of fishing, Emperor Qianlong spent most of his time at Diaoyutai perfecting his calligraphy skills. Towards the end of the Qing Dynasty, Puyi, the last emperor of China, gave Diaoyutai to his teacher Chen Baoshen as a gift.

After the People's Republic of China was established in 1949, the Diaoyutai State Guesthouse was built around the ruins of the ancient terrace. There are altogether 18 luxurious villas in this scenic area. On the National Day of 1959, Diaoyutai State Guest House was opened to guests for the first time—but not just any ordinary guest. Being a top-rate state guesthouse, it caters exclusively to foreign dignitaries. Many visiting state leaders and celebrities have stayed at the guesthouse. They include former US president Richard Nixon and Britain's Queen Elizabeth II.

LOCATION:
Diaoyutai State Guesthouse
2 Fucheng Road, Haidian District.

DITAN (The Altar of the Earth)

The temple fair at Ditan is a grand-scale event that draws massive crowds every year.

Ditan, the Altar of the Earth, represents the Chinese people's deepest gratitude for the maternal love bestowed by the earth. The ancient Chinese believed that the heaven was like their father and the earth their mother. This was a poetic portrayal of the relationship between human beings and nature in the history of civilisation.

The Chinese people believe that the earth is the source of all energies. Ditan was probably built out of this simple regard that the Chinese people had for the earth. The act of offering sacrifices to the gods that watched over the earth was the most simple—yet most loving—of all sacrificial ceremonies. It stemmed from the love and respect, instead of fear, that people had for the earth.

Ditan was built by the Ming emperors in honour of the Goddess of Earth. It is located outside Andingmen (Anding Gate). The Ming emperors also built the Altar of the Sun (Ritan) at the eastern part of Beijing and the Altar of the Moon (Yuetan) in the west of Beijing. There are also the Altar of Heaven (Tiantan) and the Altar of Land and Grain (Shejitan).

Ditan is now a park that is open to the public. It is also a venue where one of the temple fairs in Beijing is held during the Spring Festival. Ditan welcomes throngs of visitors to its temple fair and sees more tourists visiting it each year.

LOCATION:

East of Andingmenwai Dajie, Dongcheng District.

You can go there by subway, getting off at Yonghegong or Andingmen station.

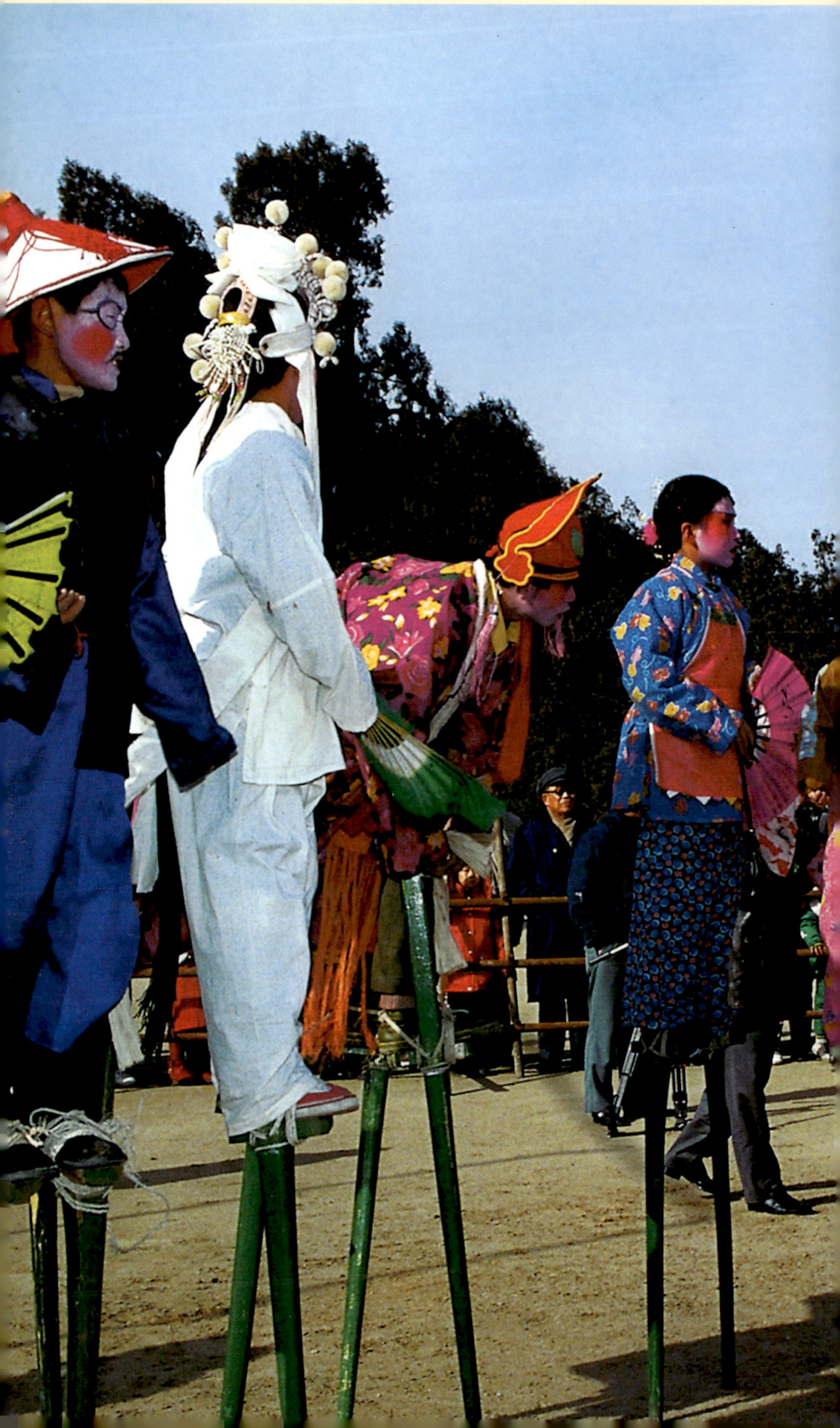

DISCOVER BEIJING   43

Walking on stilts—one of the many cultural performances at Ditan temple fair.

DONGJIAOMIN LANE

Dongjiaomin Lane was the first foreign legation quarter of China. During the Ming Dynasty, foreign diplomats and students would stay at Dongjiaomin Lane—called Dongjiangmi Lane at that time. This location was chosen because it was situated near the foreign affairs ministry. Although the Qing government had refused to establish diplomatic relations with foreign nations, it was nevertheless forced to do so after being defeated in the Second Opium War (1856–1860). Soon, countries like Britain, France, Germany, Russia and the United States all set up their embassies at Dongjiangmi Lane—establishing it as the city's earliest embassy district. It was at this time that Dongjiangmi Lane was renamed Dongjiaomin Lane.

After the Boxer Rebellion (1899–1901), China signed The Boxer Protocol with these foreign nations. In accordance with the protocol, the area of Dongjiaomin Lane was to become the legation quarter for foreign embassies. No Chinese was allowed to live in this district and the embassies could station their own troops to protect the embassies. All the Qing

This building that used to belong to the French legion is now used for commercial purposes.

government's administrative units, as well as Chinese residents, were evacuated from the area. Foreign troops were stationed in the respective embassies and cannons and high security walls were put in place.

At this restricted zone, warning signs that read "No Chinese or Dogs Allowed" could be seen. It was the very first time that such demeaning signage ever appeared in China. Troops were also stationed at the ends of Dongjiaomin Lane and they were authorised to shoot any trespassers—which of course, referred to the Chinese who defied the regulation. After several innocent people had been killed, rebels from Yihetuan (the Boxers) besieged Dongjiaomin Lane for 56 days and created great chaos.

After the People's Republic of China was established in 1949, China regained possession of Dongjiaomin Lane. The new government established new diplomatic relations with foreign nations. The areas of Yabao Road and Sanlitun were then chosen as the new embassy district.

LOCATION:
Dongcheng District. You can go there by subway, getting off at Qianmen, the nearest station.

46 DISCOVER BEIJING

Fangshan Restaurant at Qionghua Isle of Beihai Lake.

DISCOVER BEIJING 47

FANGSHAN RESTAURANT

The term '*fang shan*' refers to the reproduction of imperial cuisine. In the Qing Dynasty, the imperial kitchen was called *yu shan fang* and it prepared all the daily meals of the emperor as well as banquets for special occasions.

To the ordinary Chinese who has never had the chance to taste the dishes once served exclusively to the emperors, these delicate dishes have a legendary status. To satisfy this curiosity, Fangshan Restaurant was opened at Beihai (North Lake) Park in 1925 by Zhao Renzhai and his former colleagues—who were chefs at the imperial kitchen before the Qing government was overthrown.

Apart from the imperial kitchen, there were private kitchens for the empresses. For instance, the private kitchen of Empress Dowager Cixi was called the "West Imperial Kitchen". It took several hundred eunuchs to serve the dishes for Cixi alone. The dishes prepared by the West Imperial Kitchen were intricately prepared with rare and expensive ingredients.

Today, the extravagant dishes served by Fangshan Restaurant are also exorbitantly priced. Some of its popular dishes include baked sesame seed cake with fried minced meat filling, mashed pea cake, steamed corn-flour cake and kidney bean roll. The most popular banquet it serves is the Man-Han Banquet, which requires four to six meals—over a few days—to be completely served.

Started as a private enterprise, Fangshan Restaurant was nationalised in 1956. In 1959, it was relocated to Qionghua Isle of Beihai (North Lake) Park. It continues to win praises from its patrons for the imperial cuisine it serves.

A dish that looks as simple as this does not come with a humble price tag.

LOCATION:
Beihai Park, 1 Wenjin Jie, Xicheng District.

FAYUAN TEMPLE

LOCATION:
7 Fayuansi Qianjie, Xuanwu District.
The nearest subway station is Xuanwumen station.

Fayuan Temple is the oldest temple in Beijing. Few people actually knew of its existence if not for a novel.

Li Ao, a Taiwanese writer, had written a novel—entitled *Martyrs' Shrine: The Story of the Reform Movement of 1898 in China* (the Chinese title is *Beijing Fayuansi*)—which was nominated for the Nobel Prize in Literature in 2000. The story was set in Fayuan Temple. Overnight, it became a bestseller all across China and Taiwan. It was not long before visitors swarmed to the temple with copies of the novel in their hands.

Fayuan Temple was built in 645 by the order of Emperor Taizong (626–649) of the Tang Dynasty. The temple was originally called Minzhong Temple (Temple of Mourning the Patriots) and it was built to commemorate the soldiers who were killed in the war against the minority peoples in Northeast China. It was renamed Fayuan Temple during the reign of Emperor Yongzheng of the Qing Dynasty.

A snapshot of Fayuan Temple.

War and fire damaged the temple several times. In the great earthquake of 1057, the temple was almost completely destroyed. It was rebuilt after the earthquake and has remained intact until today.

The lilac trees of Fayuan Temple are very famous, so is the "Lilac Poets' Gathering" (*Ding Xiang Shi Hui*). Beginning from the Qing Dynasty, poets from all walks of life have assembled at Fayuan Temple for this annual gathering. In 1924, Rabindranath Tagore, the Indian poet, attended this gathering as well. However, for various reasons, the annual gathering was discontinued for 87 years until it was resumed in 2002. The Lilac Poets' Gathering is held annually in April and continues to attract poetry lovers to come together and share their love of poetry.

Fayuan Temple is now the official site of the Buddhist Academy of China.

FINANCE STREET

Beijing's Finance Street runs from Fuxingmen (Fuxing Gate) to Fuchengmen (Fucheng Gate) in the West 2nd Ring Road area. To date, more than 10 skyscrapers, including some housing the major banks of China—Commercial Bank of China, the Bank of China and the People's Bank of China—have been built along the street.

Many buildings in the Finance Street area incorporate auspicious Chinese symbolism in their design. For instance, the People's Bank of China reminds one of a Chinese *yuan bao* (shoe-shaped gold or silver ingot used as money in ancient China). Tongtai Building looks like an instrument used for measuring the weight of money in ancient times. China Construction Bank is designed based on a traditional Chinese belief that the sky is

The People's Bank of China, one of the banks located along Finance Street.

round and the earth is square. The round roof of the headquarters is built on a square base—representing the sky and the earth. The design of the Commercial Bank of China is a mixture of Chinese and Western styles. Its steel structure is Western while its inner courtyard is unquestionably Chinese.

To complement its status as an international financial hub, hotels, apartments, international schools, entertainment facilities, parks and other amenities have been built to accommodate the needs of the foreigners working in Beijing. Efforts have also been made by the Beijing State Council to ensure that the district is ecologically friendly to attract real estate investors.

With more than 95 per cent of the office area sold and leased, Finance Street is set to become a popular location for the finance and service sectors in Beijing.

LOCATION:
From Fuxingmen to Fuchengmen.
You can get there by subway, getting off at Fuxingmen station.

FORMER **EXECUTION GROUND**

Xisi was the place where public executions were carried out during the Ming Dynasty. It used to be called Xisi Archway (Xisi Pai Lou) before the archway was demolished. In the Ming Dynasty, the place was called Xishi (Western Market). It was a tradition in China to carry out executions in the marketplace to warn people of the severe consequences of committing crimes.

Many senior officials of the Ming Dynasty were executed at Xisi. Liu Jing was a eunuch and an official of Emperor Wuzong. He tried to overthrow the emperor and was executed in public. Hated by the people in the capital, he was stoned by onlookers before he was executed. After his execution, some people actually bought his flesh from the executioners and ate it.

Both Yu Qian and Yuan Chonghuan were tragic heroes of the Ming Dynasty who were also executed at Xisi.

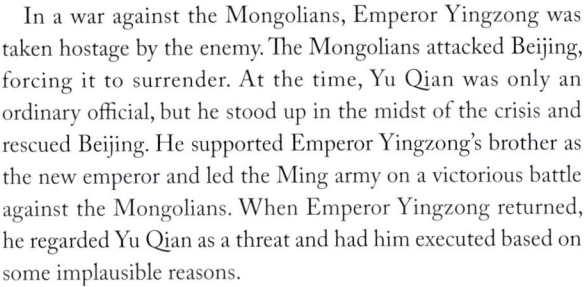

In a war against the Mongolians, Emperor Yingzong was taken hostage by the enemy. The Mongolians attacked Beijing, forcing it to surrender. At the time, Yu Qian was only an ordinary official, but he stood up in the midst of the crisis and rescued Beijing. He supported Emperor Yingzong's brother as the new emperor and led the Ming army on a victorious battle against the Mongolians. When Emperor Yingzong returned, he regarded Yu Qian as a threat and had him executed based on some implausible reasons.

The death of Yuan Chonghuan was another tragic story. Yuan was an able general of the Ming Dynasty who fought in the war against the invading Manchurians. The Manchurians then spread a rumour that Yuan was a spy. The emperor fell for the ploy and executed Yuan at Xisi.

In the Yuan Dynasty, criminals were executed in Chaishikou (Firewood Market). The execution field of the Qing Dynasty was Caishikou (Vegetable Market), which can still be found in the city map of Beijing today. Xisi Pailou is now known as Xisi Nandajie, which is still one of the busiest stretches of road in Beijing.

Where "heads rolled"—Xisi execution ground.

LOCATION:
Xisi Nandajie, Xicheng District.

FORMER INTERIM GOVERNMENT OFFICE OF **DUAN QIRUI**

Situated along Zhang Zhizhong Road is the site of the former Duan Qirui's Interim Government Office. Zhang Zhizong Road was named after an army general who died fighting the Japanese. It used to be called Tieshizi Hutong (Iron Lion Lane) after the two iron lion statues (which have been moved to the Drum Tower) that once guarded the compound.

It began its history as the residence of Tian Wan—the father of one of the concubines of the Ming emperor Chongzhen. During the Qing Dynasty, several princes also took up residence within this compound.

Towards the end of the Qing Dynasty, the residence was occupied by Guizhou School and was later demolished. A group of new Western-style buildings were then built on its site

The European-style buildings in the compound of the Former Interim Government Office of Duan Qirui.

during the reign of Emperor Guangxu. The main building in the middle is a three-storey grey brick European-style building. Three buildings stand on both sides of and opposite to the main building. Two stone lions sit at the front of the main gate.

Following the collapse of the Qing government, the Northern Warlords government located the Ministry of Navy and the Ministry of Army here. In 1912, the building became the office of President Yuan Shikai and the State Council of China. When Duan Qirui became President in 1924, he moved the government office into the building occupied by the Ministry of the Navy. It was also here that Dr Sun Yat-sen died of cancer in 1925.

What most Chinese people identify this building with is the March 18th Student Movement. On 18 March 1926, thousands of students and people from all walks of life protested in front of the building against Duan's collaboration with the Japanese, in which he was widely known to have traded Chinese territories with the Japanese for weapons. Duan ordered his troops to shoot the protesters, which resulted in 47 deaths. When the Japanese army invaded Beijing during the Sino-Japanese War, this building became the headquarters of the Japanese army in northern China.

After the People's Republic of China was established in 1949, it became the campus of the Renmin University. Now, the compound is home to Renmin University Press and China Academy of Social Sciences—among others.

LOCATION:
3 Zhangzizhong Road, Dongcheng District.

FORMER RESIDENCE OF **CAO XUEQIN**

There is a humble-looking little house in the Botanical Garden of Beijing that is the former residence of Cao Xueqin, the author of the famous classic, *Dream of the Red Chamber*. It was where Cao lived after he lost his family and fortune.

A Han Chinese by birth, Cao's great-grandfather was the Commissioner of Imperial Textiles during the Qing Dynasty. His great-grandmother was the wet nurse of Emperor Kangxi and his grandfather was the young emperor's playmate. Earning Emperor Kangxi's trust, Cao's family prospered during his reign and the title of Commissioner of Imperial Textiles was later inherited by Cao's grandfather and father. However, during the

The much debated Cao Xueqin's inscriptions on the walls of his residence.

early years of Emperor Yongzheng's reign, the family was caught up in a political tussle and the family properties were confiscated. Cao's family was then relocated in Beijing.

Living all by himself, Cao spent 10 years writing *Dream of the Red Chamber*. Two hundred years later, when locals were renovating the house, they found many poems written on the wall. Scholars studied the content and the handwriting of these poems and decided that the poems were Cao's works. That was how the former residence of Cao Xueqin was discovered.

Today, the furnishings of the living quarters and the study in the house have been left untouched since Cao lived in it. The poems still remain on the wall. It evokes the impression that Cao still lives there today. However, some scholars are doubtful whether Cao Xueqin had actually lived in it. It is questionable too that this little house has remained in such good condition for 200 years whereas other houses built in the same period have all fallen into disrepair.

Scholars also pointed out that most of the poems on the wall were copied from pulp fiction popular during the Ming Dynasty. A scholar like Cao could not have been a lover of such works—let alone inscribing them on the walls. Another point was raised on the unscientific methods used in authenticating Cao Xueqin's handwriting.

Regardless of all these debatable points, the former residence of Cao Xueqin is still adored by lovers of the novel, *Dream of the Red Chamber*. The significant fact is that Cao Xueqin was indeed a resident in Beijing. Whether Cao Xueqin had really lived in this little house at the foot of Fragrant Hills was of little consequence.

A sculpture of Cao Xueqin at the Former Residence of Cao Xueqin.

LOCATION:
39 Zhengbaiqi (inside Beijing Botanical Garden), Xiangshan, Haidian District.

FORMER RESIDENCE OF PRINCE GONG

Prince Gong's mansion is tucked amidst lavish greenery.

Prince Gong's mansion occupies a land area of more than 16 acres and is located on the east bank of Shichahai (Shicha Lake). It is about the same size as Zhongshan Park and is notably the most lavishly decorated and well-preserved prince's mansion in Beijing. And the person responsible for such lavishness was none other than Heshen, the notoriously corrupt prime minister of Emperor Qianlong.

During Emperor Qianlong's reign, this courtyard mansion was given to Heshen, his trusted prime minister who rose rapidly to power from a mere sedan-chair bearer for the emperor. Heshen was the father of the emperor's son-in-law and as the first owner of the mansion, he was also rumoured to be the emperor's gay lover. Hence, although Heshen was notorious for his arrogance, corrupt practices and affluent lifestyle, he enjoyed unrivalled power and prestige during Qianlong's reign.

Heshen amassed so much wealth through his corrupt practices that he could spend lavishly on enlarging and decorating his mansion—in a style that could rival that of the imperial family. When Emperor Qianlong died, the succeeding emperor Jiaqing executed Heshen and confiscated all his possessions on charges of corruption.

After eliminating Heshen, Emperor Jiaqing gave his courtyard mansion to Prince Qing. Subsequently, it was owned by Prince Gong—from whom the courtyard mansion got its name. Prince Gong assisted Empress Dowager Cixi in securing her power in the imperial court. However, instead of becoming a trusted official of Cixi, he was regarded as a political threat and was dismissed by the suspicious Cixi.

Prince Gong's mansion was so huge that one of its gardens was used as a part of the Peking University campus. Even the stable of the mansion was so magnificent that it was converted into a residential compound—occupied by Guo Moruo, the famous writer and former vice premier of China.

LOCATION:

14 Liuyin Jie, Xicheng District

You can get there by subway. The nearest station is Gulou Dajie.

FORMER RESIDENCE OF SONG QINGLING

Former residence of Song Qingling. The former residence of Song Qingling is a big courtyard mansion located to the north of Houhai. The first owner of the mansion was Mingzhu, a minister of Emperor Kangxi's. During Emperor Qianlong's reign (1736–1795), the descendants of Mingzhu offended a high-ranking minister. The house was then confiscated by the imperial court and Heshen, Qianlong's favourite minister, took possession of it as one of his mansions. When Heshen was executed, the mansion was given to Prince Yongxing. Later, it was given to Prince Chun.

When Prince Chun's second son Guangxu became emperor, Prince Chun moved out of this house. This was in accordance with the tradition that the houses in which emperors lived before their enthronement were not to be allowed for residential purposes. From 1963 to 1981, the mansion was occupied by Song Qingling—the wife of Dr Sun Yat-sen.

The mansion occupied an area of about 5 hectares. It can be roughly divided into three sections. The main structure is the central section. The eastern section was made up of an ancestral temple and a Buddhist temple. The western section included a study room.

Prince Chun was probably the most celebrated man of his time. He married the sister of Empress Dowager Cixi and both his son and grandson became emperors. His grandson Puyi was the last emperor of China.

In 1912, Sun Yat-sen visited this mansion when he came to Beijing. His widow Song Qingling became the vice-chairman of China's Communist Party after the founding of the People's Republic of China in 1949. Song then lived in the western garden of this mansion from 1963 to 1981. This western garden is now a residential museum as a memorial to Song Qingling.

Of all the former residences of princes in Beijing, only the mansions of Prince Chun and Prince Gong are open to the public.

LOCATION:

46 Houhaibeiyan, Xicheng District.

You can get there by subway, getting off at Jishuitan station.

GRAND VIEW GARDEN (Daguanyuan)

A scene from Dream of the Red Chamber that is performed at Grand View Garden daily.

Grand View Garden is located in the south of Beijing. It is a replica of the Daguanyuan mansion as depicted in the novel *Dream of the Red Chamber* by Cao Xueqin, a Qing Dynasty writer. The story is set in the Ming Dynasty and tells of a noble family who live in a big courtyard mansion called Daguanyuan.

Grand View Park was originally a temporary garden used as the set for the filming of the TV series *Dream of the Red Chamber*—an adaptation of the novel—in 1984. Upon completion of the filming, the Xuanwu District Government decided to convert the film set into a scenic spot.

The project cost roughly 4 million yuan and took several years to complete. The chief concern was that the garden be as close as possible to the description of the Grand View Mansion in the novel. Hence, experts in the study of the novel were involved in its design and landscaping.

The nobles in the Qing Dynasty usually had very large houses with gardens. By comparison, Grand View Garden—as a faithful replica—is only but a miniature version of what the actual garden in the classical novel would have been.

LOCATION:
12 Nancaiyuan Jie, Xuanwu District.

GUOZIJIAN (The Imperial College)

Guozijian is located on Guozijian Street inside Andingmen (Anding Gate). It was the highest institution of learning in China for more than 600 years.

Guozijian was first built in 1306 during the Yuan Dynasty and was rebuilt several times during the Ming Dynasty and the Qing Dynasty. Yilun Hall (the principal's office), Dacheng Palace and all the stone tablets were built at that time. Piyong Palace is the principal building of Guozijian. It was very famous in Beijing and was one of the "Six Best Palaces" of Beijing. Piyong Palace was constructed during the reign of Emperor Qianlong of the Qing Dynasty.

During the Ming and Qing dynasties, the imperial examinations were held once every three years, with 51,624 candidates successfully passing the examinations. There is a stele in Guozijian on which the names of all these candidates are engraved. The last imperial examination was held towards the end of the Qing Dynasty in 1904.

The principal of Guozijian was called *Ji Jiu* in Chinese and the students were called *Jian Sheng*. It was considered a privilege to be admitted into Guozijian as the students could still find employment easily in the county governments outside the capital even if they did not manage to pass the examinations. In fact, many of them stayed in Beijing and worked as secretaries in the central government.

Guozijian also received foreign students from Japan, Korea, Vietnam, Russia and other countries, which helped in fostering cultural exchange between China and foreign countries.

Towards the end of the Qing Dynasty, the renowned status of Guozijian and its students declined. Graduates of Guozijian could no longer find jobs in county governments. People who never attended Guozijian could even purchase the diplomas issued by Guozijian and claim themselves as graduates of the college.

Since the founding of the People's Republic of China in 1949, Guozijian has been home to the Capital Library.

The archway at Guozijian Imperial College.

LOCATION:
13 Guozijian Jie, Dongcheng District. You can get there by subway, getting off at Yonghegong station.

DISCOVER BEIJING 63

HUANGCHENGGEN

Before the 1900s, many relatives of the emperor and government officials lived in the vicinity of the Forbidden City. Therefore, the lifestyle in the neighbourhood was very aristocratic. Today, you can still see several former residences of princes and high officials of the Qing Dynasty in this neighbourhood.

The Manchurians conquered the whole of China and founded the Qing Dynasty in 1644. At that time, the city of Beijing was divided into the inner and the outer city. The emperor lived in the Forbidden City, which is located in the centre of Beijing. The inner city was the neighbourhood around the Forbidden City. As this area was crucial to the safety of the emperor, the Han people were driven out of the inner city but were allowed to take residence in the outer city.

The emperor's relatives, officials and the "Eight Banners" (military organisation of the Manchurians) resided in the inner city. The emperor's relatives received a monthly allowance from the emperor. They did not have to work and lived extravagantly. They spent their time watching Chinese operas and keeping pets such as birds, goldfish and crickets. When the Qing Dynasty was overthrown and replaced by the Republic of China, these imperial relatives lost their income, but they carried on with their extravagant way of life.

After the founding of the People's Republic of China in 1949, they lost their ties with the imperial court, but the culture they created is still found in the neighbourhood around the Forbidden City.

For instance, there is a market near Nanheyan Street that was once their favourite haunt. The shops there sell everything from birds and fish to curios. In this market, visitors can buy souvenirs that truly represent the culture of Beijing. Most of the antiques sold here are authentic.

While this market has seen better days when the rich aristocrats visited in search of rare finds, visitors today are mainly window shoppers.

LOCATION:
Southwest of the Forbidden City.

You can walk around the Forbidden City to experience the feeling of Huangchenggen.

DISCOVER BEIJING 65

Part of the original inner city wall.

HUTONG

The term '*hutong*' first came into being during the Yuan Dynasty. It originally means 'well' in Mongolian. Then people started using the word to refer to small streets or lanes near the well. There was probably a well in every street or lane in the city at that time.

In the past, people usually lived near a well. Besides providing water, wells also performed a very important social function in people's everyday life. People who lived in courtyard houses were very much isolated from the world and they hardly had the chance to communicate with their neighbours. Meeting at the well gave them an opportunity to socialise with one another.

In Beijing, there are stories behind almost every *hutong*. To the west of Wangfujing Street is a lane called Dongchang Hutong. The lane got its name from Dongchang (National Security Institution) that was situated nearby.

Dongchang was the first National Security Institution set up in 1421 by Emperor Yongle of the Ming Dynasty. The eunuchs put in charge of Dongchang were notorious for arresting innocent people and torturing them to admit to crimes they did not commit. The people in the capital were terrified of these eunuchs. Dongchang Hutong thus became one of the most-feared lanes in Beijing during the Ming Dynasty.

The Foreign Ministry Street near Dongdan was once called Shidaren Hutong (His Excellency Shi's Lane). Shi Heng was a general of the Ming Dynasty. He had assisted Prince Yingzong in overthrowing his brother, Emperor Jingzong. When Yingzong became emperor, he gave Shi Heng a big courtyard mansion, which surpassed many princes' mansions in its grandeur.

Years later, Shi was accused of treason and the mansion was confiscated. But the lane where the mansion was located was called Shidaren Hutong until 1949. In the 1910s, a state guesthouse was built at the site of Shi Heng's house. Yuan Shikai, president of China at that time, once held office there. On 24 August 1912, Sun Yat-sen stayed in this guesthouse when he visited Beijing.

A small lane in Dongcheng District called Gongxian Hutong (Bowstring Lane) has a "Half-Acre Garden" (Banmuyuan) in this lane designed by Li Yu, a famous novelist and dramatist.

The gate of a courtyard house is decorated with a door stone (mendun).

This made Gongxian Hutong famous. Many lanes were named after celebrities of the time and became famous because of their association with these celebrities.

Tieshizi Hutong (Iron Lion Lane) is a wide lane. Lanes like Erduoyanr Lane (Ear and Eye Lane) are very narrow. The narrowest spot of Qianshi Lane (Money Market Lane) is only 0.4 metres wide. The widest stretch of this lane is 0.8 metres.

68 DISCOVER BEIJING

DISCOVER BEIJING   69

Many lanes were renamed after the People's Republic of China was established in 1949. Dayaba Hutong (Big Dummy Lane) became Dayabao Hutong (Big Treasure Lane). Wangguafu Hutong (Widow Wang Lane) was renamed Wangguangfu Hutong (Grand Happiness Lane).

Visitors to Beijing should include a "*hutong* tour" as part of their itinerary. Only by visiting them can one catch a glimpse of the lifestyle of the common people in Beijing.

Tourists who find walking a chore can visit the *hutong* in one of these rickshaws.

JINGHANG GRAND CANAL

Jinghang Grand Canal runs from Tongzhou—to the east of Beijing—to Hangzhou of Zhejiang Province. It cuts across Beijing, Tianjin, Hebie, Shandong, Jiangsu and Zhejiang and measures 1,794 kilometres in length. With a history of more than 2,400 years, it is one of the oldest man-made canals—and also the longest—ever built.

This pagoda once served as the lighthouse of Jinghang Grand Canal.

The oldest section of the Grand Canal dates back to the 5th Century B.C. Construction began during the Spring and Autumn period when the Duke of Wu ordered a canal to be built for his conquest of the northern kingdoms. Over the next couple of centuries, additional sections of the Grand Canal were connected and during the Sui Dynasty, when the capital was located in Luoyang, an order was given by the emperor to link Beijing and Hangzhou via the Grand Canal.

The canal was used mainly to transport grain and other commodities from the southern Chinese provinces to Beijing. This brought about the economic development of the area around the Grand Canal—which became vibrant business centres during that time. Tongzhou, a county to the east of Beijing, was an example. The city prospered after the canal was constructed but once trains started to transport goods at a much faster rate, the canal fell into disuse and this greatly affected the economy of Tongzhou as well.

The section of the canal that ran from Tongzhou to Tianjin was known as the Northern Grand Canal. It was also called Lu River. For thousands of years, food and other commodities were transported to Tongzhou via the Grand Canal.

As a city, everything Beijing needed was imported via the Grand Canal. Every year, 20,000 shiploads of food were transported from southern China to Beijing. Even building materials such as tiles and wood were imported from the south. Other than food and other essential commodities, the Grand Canal also brought about cultural exchanges between the north and south of China. It left an impression on foreign visitors such as the Italian traveller Marco Polo and the Roman Catholic missionary Matteo Ricci, who saw the Grand Canal in its more prosperous days.

DISCOVER BEIJING 71

JING SHAN PARK (Scenery Hill)

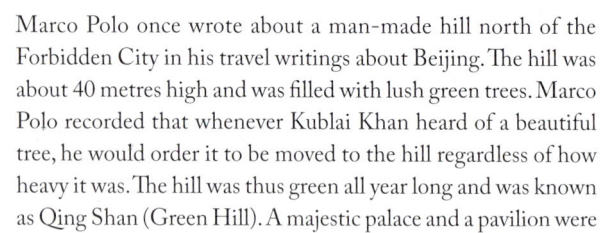

Marco Polo once wrote about a man-made hill north of the Forbidden City in his travel writings about Beijing. The hill was about 40 metres high and was filled with lush green trees. Marco Polo recorded that whenever Kublai Khan heard of a beautiful tree, he would order it to be moved to the hill regardless of how heavy it was. The hill was thus green all year long and was known as Qing Shan (Green Hill). A majestic palace and a pavilion were later built on the top of the hill.

This man-made hill is actually called Jing Shan (Scenery Hill). Some historians believed that the hill mentioned by Marco Polo was actually on Qionghua Isle in the middle of Beihai (North Lake). The palace was Guanghan Palace, which was destroyed during the Ming Dynasty. Others pointed out that the hill should be Mei Shan, which means "Coal Hill".

In actual fact, Jing Shan had several names. In the Ming Dynasty, it was called Changshou Shan (Longevity Hill). Then how did it get the name "Mei Shan"? Some people believed that coal was once stored deep under the hill for emergency. Others thought that the hill got this name because coal used to be piled up at the foot of the hill.

Jing Shan is the best place to take in a bird's eye view of the city. In the old days when there were no skyscrapers in Beijing, no building was higher than Jing Shan although it was only 44 metres high. The best place to take in the sight of the Forbidden City was from the pavilion on Jing Shan, which was closest to the northern part of the city wall. Looking out, the magnificence of the Forbidden City was in clear view. When the sky was clear, one could even see the walls of the outer city at the distance. But that was in the past. After the founding of the People's Republic of China in 1949, the walls of the inner city and the outer city were all demolished.

Jing Shan also had a defence role. Qianmen (Qian Gate), Tian'anmen (Tian'an Gate) and Jing Shan were all built along the same central axis as the Forbidden City. It was located to the north of all these gates. Hence, Jing Shan was the best place to monitor the beacon towers on the Great Wall.

The last Ming emperor Chongzhen ascended the throne when he was 18. Unfortunately, it was a time when the great dynasty

Jing Shan Park in winter.

DISCOVER BEIJING 73

was on the verge of collapse. On 19 March 1644, the rebel Li Zicheng occupied Beijing with his peasant troops in the peasant uprising. Defeated, Emperor Chongzhen killed his wife and daughter before hanging himself on a tree on Jing Shan.

Before he died, Chongzhen wrote his last imperial edict on his clothes—in which he lamented how his ministers and officials had deceived him. Before fleeing the palace, he made a last bid to summon help from his officials but no one came to his aid. Only one eunuch accompanied him to Jing Shan and committed suicide together with Emperor Chongzhen. The original tree was subsequently destroyed and a new one has been planted to mark the site of the suicide.

The area around Jing Shan was rebuilt into a park and has been open to the public since 1928. It is now a popular scenic spot in Beijing, attracting visitors from all walks of life.

LOCATION:
1 Wenjin Street, Xicheng District.

KUNMING LAKE

Kunming Lake was originally called West Lake, which is the name of a number of lakes in China. The West Lake in Hangzhou is probably the most famous of them.

During the Yuan Dynasty, Kublai Khan assigned Guo Shoujing to connect the different parts of the Jinghang Grand Canal. Guo channelled waters into the canal from Jade Spring Hill (Yuquan Hill) through Wangshanpo Lake. Wangshanpo Lake then served as a reservoir for the canal. Later, it was given the name "West Lake". A long causeway called the "West Causeway" was built across the lake. Every April, visitors swarmed to the lakeside to enjoy the beautiful scenery.

In the Qing Dynasty, Emperor Qianlong chose this scenic spot for the construction of an imperial garden for his mother. He then renamed Wong Hill—located near the lake—as Longevity Hill (Changshou Shan). Emperor Qianlong also

The impressive Kunming Lake.

had the lake enlarged eastward and renamed it Kunming Lake. The West Causeway was renamed East Causeway. As it was an imperial garden, commoners were forbidden to visit the lake from then on.

Empress Dowager Cixi spent a lavish sum on the reconstruction of the lake and built the Summer Palace (Yiheyuan) there. It was also there that she spent most of her time, instead of at the Forbidden City.

The Long Corridor in the Summer Palace is famous for the paintings on its beams. Some of the paintings are of birds and flowers; others depict scenes from Chinese literary classics. These paintings by unknown artists of the Qing Dynasty have outlived the emperors and survived till the present day.

DISCOVER BEIJING

LIULICHANG

One of the antique shops in Liulichang Street.

Liulichang Street is known for its wide selection of antiques, handicrafts and Chinese paintings. It was once a small village called Haiwangcun (King of the Sea Village). In the Ming Dynasty, kilns were built in this village to make glazed roof tiles for the construction of imperial palaces. The names of many locations in the area, such as Shatuyuan (Garden of Sand and Stone) or Liulijing (Well of Glazed Tile), are reminders of its history.

The kilns were relocated in 1544 during the Ming Dynasty. At the beginning of the Qing Dynasty, many guildhalls were built near Liulichang Street and various booksellers started their businesses in the street. Soon, the area became a cultural street where visitors could also shop for items such as writing brushes, ink, paper, antiques and paintings. When Emperor Qianlong ordered the compilation of *Siku Quanshu* (*Complete Library of the Four Branches of Literature*), the 15,000 scholars who worked on it frequently gathered in the guildhalls near Liulichang Street, which became a convenient place for them to purchase and sell books.

Today at Liulichang Street visitors can find old books, paintings and antiques, as well as papers, writing brushes and seals for Chinese calligraphy. Popular among many local and foreign visitors is Rongbaozhai Studio, which is famous for its woodblock printing and reproductions of traditional Chinese paintings.

LOCATION:
Xuanwu District.

Immerse yourself in the world of antiques at Liulichang Street.

LONG CORRIDOR

The Long Corridor at Summer Palace.

The Long Corridor at the Summer Palace (Yiheyuan) was built in 1750. It starts from Yaoyuemen (the Gate of Invitation to the Moon) in the east and ends at Shizhang Pavilion.

The Long Corridor lies in front of Longevity Hill (Wanshoushan) with four double-eaved octagonal pavilions alongside it. The names of the four pavilions are Liujia, Jilan, Qiushui and Qingyao. They represent the four seasons of the year. These four pavilions connect the different parts of the Long Corridor.

This a clever design, such that when people walk along the Long Corridor, they seldom notice the change of direction and height. There are more than 14,000 paintings on the beams of the corridor and it is frequently referred to as the "Corridor of Paintings".

Some of the paintings depict characters and scenes from classical novels such as *Romance of the Three Kingdoms*, *Outlaws of the Marsh*, *Dream of the Red Chamber*, *Creation of the Gods* and *Romance of the Western Bower*. All these paintings are works of artists who lived more than 300 years ago.

Over time, some paintings have been damaged. Although the institution in charge of the Summer Palace has engaged a group of specialists and artists to restore all the damaged paintings, some scholars are against such repair but it seems the only way to protect these paintings.

LONGFU TEMPLE

Longfu Temple survives only in name and is now non-existent. On the former site of the temple is Longfu Plaza—a modern shopping complex complete with elevators and air-conditioning. Not many people know about the past existence of the temple and its temple fair.

Longfu Temple was built in 1425. During the Ming Dynasty it was the only temple where both Tibetan Buddhists and traditional Chinese Buddhists coexisted in a time when the two sects were known to be bitter rivals. During the Qing Dynasty, Longfu Temple was strictly for the consecration of Tibetan Buddhism. It stored many Buddhist scriptures and it was more popular than Yonghegong Temple.

The archway that is the closest reminder of Longfusi Temple.

The temple fair held at Longfu Temple was probably the largest in Beijing during the Ming and Qing dynasties. It was even held regularly on the 1st, 2nd, 9th and 10th day of the month during the Qing Dynasty. At the fairs, vendors sold all kinds of traditional Chinese snacks. Toys made of clay, wood and bamboo attracted the attention of the children. There were martial arts performances and magic shows.

After the founding of the People's Republic of China in 1949, the temple fair ceased operation and was replaced by an outdoor market. Longfu Temple became the storehouse of the market goods. In the 1960s, Longfu Temple became a department store known as Dongsi People's Department Store.

During the Cultural Revolution, Longfu Temple was completely demolished. Longfu Plaza was built at the site of the temple during the "Reform and Opening-up" movement of the 1980s. It soon became one of the four major department stores of Beijing—probably because there were few department stores in Beijing then.

In 1993, Longfu Plaza burned down in a fire. Although it was rebuilt, business at Longfu Plaza did not pick up as many shopping complexes and supermarkets had begun to spring up in Beijing.

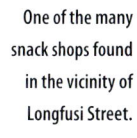

One of the many snack shops found in the vicinity of Longfusi Street.

LOCATION:
Longfusi Jie, Dongcheng District.

MAN-HAN BANQUET

The Manchurians led a simple life in Manchuria. During mealtimes, the chieftains usually sat on the ground around a fire. But after conquering China and settling in the capital city Beijing, they quickly adopted the etiquette of the Han people.

The Manchurians always kept a wary eye on the Han people. In the imperial palace, when the Qing emperors hosted a dinner for their ministers and officials, the Manchurian and Han ministers were seated separately. Gradually, the rules were relaxed and the Han ministers could be seated with their Manchurian counterparts at imperial banquets.

Usually, the hundreds of guests would be treated to the finest cuisine comprising more than a hundred different dishes. The feast is called "Man-Han Banquet". It became so popular that the rich in China began to serve a similar banquet.

Across China, the menus of Man-Han Banquet are quite different, with the Man-Han Banquet of Yangzhou famed to be the best. The ingredients used in preparing the dishes are all rare and expensive. The banquet usually takes one to three days to finish and carries on for the entire day with intervals for the guests to rest. The "dinner" is finished only after all of the more than one hundred dishes have been completely served.

Today, the Man-Han Banquet is an attraction to the foreigners. Many people visit Beijing only to savour the exquisite dishes of the banquet, which is offered at well-known restaurants that serve imperial cuisine.

You may savour the Man-han Banquet at Fangshan Restaurant (see details at Fangshan Restaurant entry).

A small fraction of what one will get to savour at the Manchurian-Han Banquet.

MING TOMBS

When the Ming Emperor Zhu Di ordered the construction of the Forbidden City and moved the Chinese capital from Nanjing to Beijing, he also ordered the construction of a grand tomb called Chang Tomb in Changping, the northeast suburban area of Beijing. It was a massive tomb and its sweeping scale was comparable to Xiao Tomb of the first Qing emperor.

The construction of Chang Tomb, which encompassed the rampart, the actual tomb, the squared town, and the underground grave, began during the 7th year (1409) of Zhu Di's reign and took four years to complete.

The main building in Chang Tomb is En Temple and it was meant for sacrificial rites. It is the biggest wooden construction in the Ming Dynasty and in terms of size, Taihe Hall in the Forbidden City is nowhere in comparison. Chang Tomb has the longest corridor, the biggest stele and stele pavilion and the grandest memorial temple among the 13 Ming Tombs that were built during the Ming Dynasty.

Many valuable items like gold, jade and brocade were buried together with the bodies of the emperors. It is commonly believed that these tombs house untold treasures. In Ding Tomb (Ding Ling) of Emperor Wanli, which was unearthed in 1956, archaeologists found many luxury items: 160 pieces of brocade, the emperor and the empress's crowns and gowns with hundreds of precious stones and thousands of pearls—to name just a few.

The only Ming Tomb that has been unearthed and open to visitors is the Ding Tomb, which is only a mid-size tomb among the Ming Tombs. However, it took 28 days for 20,000 labourers to move a huge slab of stone from Fangshan in the southwest of Beijing to the northwest of the capital for the construction of the tomb's gate. According to historical records, Xian Tomb—the comparatively small-scale tomb—took 23,000 soldiers and craftsmen to build. Even the smallest Jing Tomb had required 10,000 labourers for its construction.

The Ming Tombs could be considered as the "Underground Forbidden City". Its location was selected no less carefully than that of the Forbidden City itself. The area chosen for the construction of all the 13 Tombs was based on *fengshui* principles.

84　DISCOVER BEIJING

DISCOVER BEIJING 85

LOCATION:
Changping District, Beijing.
You can take the tourist buses at Qianmen & Beijing Railway Station to get there.

The Ming Tombs are completely enclosed by mountains, quiet valleys and tranquil waters, which are essential elements that constitute a good *fengshui* alignment that not only wards off evil forces, but is also believed to bring lasting blessings to one's descendants.

These sculptures of sacred creatures grace the passageway where the Ming rulers were escorted to their final resting place.

MUSEUMS OF BEIJING

The museums of a city are its storehouses of memory. There are more than 100 museums in Beijing. Together, these museums form the cultural part of the city. Both local residents and foreign visitors enjoy visiting these museums.

To the east of the Tian'anmen Square, the National Museum of China (the combination of the former National Museum of Chinese History and National Museum of Chinese Revolution) exhibits the historical artefacts of China. To the west of the Tian'anmen Square is the Great Hall of the People (Legislature of China).

Besides the National Museum of China and the Museum of the Forbidden City, the other museums in Beijing fall into four categories. The first is of museums of historical figures. The most famous ones are the Museum of Chairman Mao, the Museum of Lu Xun, Song Qingling's Former Residence, the Museum of Guo Moruo, and the Museum of Mei Lanfang. Other museums include the Museum of Li Dazhao, the Museum of Guo Shoujing, the Museum of Wu Yunduo and the Museum of Cao Xueqin.

The second is of museums of particular fields in science and technology, sports and the arts. The National Art Museum of China and the Museum of Sports are two famous museums of this nature. In Beijing, people can find museums of military technology, geology, space technology, agriculture, paleontology, ethnic culture, astronomy, nature, ancient bells, stone carvings, ancient architecture, ancient observatory, the Great Wall, ancient coins, printing technology and stamps.

The third is of museums of tombs, temples and former residences of princes. They include the Ming Tombs, White Pagoda Temple, Yonghegong Temple, Zhengyangmen, Zhonggulou Tower, Fahai Temple, Dajue Temple, Cibei Temple and the former residence of Prince Gong. These museums offer visitors a glimpse of the lifestyle of the people in the past.

The last category is of museums, such as the Museum of the Sino-Japanese War, built to commemorate historic events. In recent years, some private museums have also appeared in Beijing. There is a Museum of Old Furniture and a museum exhibiting and selling furniture made of sandalwood. These museums are smaller and more professionally run.

The National Art Museum.

NATIONAL **GRAND THEATRE**

Shortly after the People's Republic of China was established in 1949, former premier Zhou Enlai proposed that a national grand theatre be built to the west of the Great Hall of People. As China was unable to afford such a project at that time, the idea was shelved.

In the 1980s and 1990s, the proposal to build a national grand theatre resurfaced. After a period of deliberation, the State Council decided in 1997 that a national theatre would be built and a special committee in charge of the construction of the theatre was established.

In 1998, the committee came up with three criteria for the design of the National Grand Theatre. First, it should be a typical theatre. Second, it should be a Chinese theatre. Third, it should blend in with the landscape of Tian'anmen Square nearby. Many architects felt that those three criteria were contradictory. In general, they believed that the theatre should be a modern piece of architecture that was compatible with its surroundings.

In July 1998, 44 proposed designs were displayed at the Historical Museum of China. On 3 August 1998, five designs were short-listed by the State Council. By the end of 1998, it was decided that French architect Paul Andreu would design the new National Grand Theatre. In Andreu's design, the egg-shaped theatre would house three performance halls under its titanium-clad dome. The theatre is 200,000 square metres in size with a seating capacity of 6,500 people.

Construction began in the spring of 1999 but was halted due to budget problems. Construction resumed in 2001 and it was targeted to be completed in three years. However, its construction took an additional two years and was completed in 2006.

The National Grand Theatre.

LOCATION:
West side of the Great Hall of the People, Tian'anmen Square.

You can get there by subway, getting off at Tian'anmenxi station.

PAGODA

There are four white pagodas in Beijing that are worth mentioning. They are located at Miaoying Temple, Huang Temple, Qionghua Isle in Beihai Park and on the peak of Yuquan Hill. These white pagodas are also known as Lama pagodas.

The impact of minority races in Beijing is apparent. During the Yuan Dynasty, Tibetan Buddhism or the Lama Sect was the national religion. It was at this time that the Lama pagodas, which are distinctively white in colour and resemble the shape of Buddha in meditation, took root in Beijing. The largest white pagoda in Beijing was constructed in the compound of Miaoying Temple in 1271, the 8th year of Kublai Khan's reign.

Emperors of the Qing Dynasty attached great importance to Tibetan Buddhism as well. The Lama pagodas built in Beijing during the Qing Dynasty were no fewer than the ones built in the Yuan Dynasty.

Huang Temple was a famous Tibetan Buddhist temple built during the Qing Dynasty. It was where Tibetan officials and Lamas stayed when they visited Beijing. The white pagoda in Huang Temple was built in honour of the 6th Dalai Lama, who passed away when he visited Beijing in 1780 to attend Emperor Qianlong's birthday celebration.

The white pagoda at Beihai (North Lake) was built during the reign of Emperor Shunzhi. It has become so popular in Beijing that it is now one of the symbols of the city.

The Miaogao white pagoda on Yuquan Hill, located in the western suburb of Beijing, was constructed during the early years of Emperor Qianlong's reign. What makes it stand out from the other Lama pagodas are the glazed tiles used to decorate it.

However, the pagodas of Beijing are not entirely Lama pagodas. For instance, the Wansonglaoren Pagoda at Zhuanta Lane—built during the Yuan Dynasty—is a seven-level pentagonal brick pagoda which is not a typical Lama pagoda.

The difference in architectural style is also evident in the seven pagodas found near the ruins of old Yansheng Temple at Yin Shan (Silver Mountain) in the north of Changping County. Dating back to the Jin Dynasty (1115–1231) and Yuan Dynasty, these pagodas are also not in the style of a Lama pagoda.

LOCATION:
Visit Beihai Park to see the white pagoda.
1 Weijing Street, Xicheng District.

One of the white pagodas in Beijing.

DISCOVER BEIJING 91

PANJIAYUAN MARKET

It is said that are three things every visitor to Beijing must do: visit the Great Wall, savour Peking roast duck and visit the Panjiayuan Market.

Panjiayuan Market is the largest antique market in Beijing and probably the largest in China as well. It started in 1992 as a small flea market on Jinsongnan Road in Chaoyang District. The market became very popular and in 1995, it moved to its permanent address at Panjiayuan.

Visitors can buy almost everything at Panjiayuan Market. The commodities sold here include replicas of Ming and Qing-dynasty furniture, calligraphy, jewellery, ceramic

Search for rare finds at Panjiayuan Market.

wares, coins, Buddhist statues, ethnic clothes and Cultural Revolution memorabilia. However, most of the antiques sold in this market are replicas and are mass-produced. Very few antiques are real and buyers have to be experts in picking out the real stuff.

In recent years, the market has become increasingly famous. As more foreign visitors shop at Panjiayuan Market, vendors have even started picking up the English language.

On Saturdays and Sundays, the market opens at 4:30 in the morning, hence, Panjiayuan Market is also called "Ghost Market". Customers who shop with torches in their hands are certainly old-timers who know the tradition of bringing along torches when visiting Panjiayuan Market before dawn.

LOCATION:
16 Huaweilu, Chaoyang District.

PEKING OPERA AND MEI LANFANG

People in old Beijing spent most of their leisure time in teahouses and theatres. They were venues where Peking opera was staged. Peking opera was not so highly regarded back in the olden days as it is now. It was considered a popular form of entertainment just like today's movies. Opera lovers of that time enjoyed Peking opera as they did gardening or rearing birds and fish. It was typical for people in old Beijing to regard such a solemn art in such a casual manner.

It has been more than 200 years since the Anhui opera troupes first came to Beijing. Anhui opera is believed to be the origin of Peking opera. Originally, these opera troupes performed in the palace as entertainment for the imperial family but it gradually became a form of public entertainment. Peking opera has gone through half a century of evolution following its introduction in Beijing and has integrated various kinds of Chinese operas to become what it is today.

Peking opera involves four main roles: *sheng* (male role), *dan* (female role), *jing* (painted face male role) and *chou* (clown, male or female role). The different roles represent opposite qualities of good vs evil, beautiful vs ugly, etc.

The repertoire of Peking opera usually centres on civil and political events in China's history and tells the stories of kings, generals, ministers and great beauties—all of which the Chinese people are familiar with.

Peking opera has created an era of star actors who won the hearts of audience with their aria, acting and stage gaits. They were idolised for bringing ancient heroes to life. In their performances, these actors were immortalised as well.

In general, the difficult role in Peking opera is the *dan* role. This female role was traditionally performed by male actors. Mei Lanfang, Cheng Yanqiu, Shang Xiaoyun and Xun Huisheng were four popular *dan* performers who were immortalised for the *dan* roles they so expertly performed. Among them, Mei Lanfang (1894–1961) was hailed as the "Grand Master" of Peking opera.

Mei Lanfang (1894–1961) was not only a highly accomplished Peking opera actor in the three main components of Peking opera, namely singing, dancing and acting, but he also revolutionalised

The Peking Opera face masks—representing different characters.

the way Peking opera was traditionally performed. He created his very own style in performing Peking opera and gave birth to the "Mei School". He was also actively involved in writing new plays and choreographing—many of which became his legacy to Peking opera.

Most notably, Mei Lanfang was credited for being the first performer to introduce Peking opera overseas. He brought Peking opera to audiences in the United States, the former Soviet Union and Japan and was greatly recognised for the impact he created in the world of performance arts.

For his artistic achievement and contribution to cultural exchange between China and other countries, he was conferred the honorary degree of Doctor of Letters by two American universities, Pomona College and the University of Southern California. After the founding of the People's Republic of China in 1949, he served as the director of China Peking Opera Theatre and the Institute of Chinese Opera Research and the vice-chairman of China Federation of Literary and Art Circles.

Visitors to Beijing who are keen to learn more about Mei Lanfang can visit the Mei Lanfang Memorial Museum located at Huguosi Street. It is Mei's former residence and on exhibit are Mei's personal collection of books, manuscripts, calligraphy and paintings, costumes that he had donned and photographs that document his illustrious life.

LOCATION:
Meilanfang Memorial Museum.
9 Huguosi Jie, Xicheng District.

PEKING **ROAST DUCK**

The most famous dish in Beijing is probably Peking roast duck. Tourists who have not tasted such a delicacy would find their visit incomplete. Peking roast duck has really become the trademark of Beijing. Many tourists come to Beijing in the hope of visiting the Forbidden City, the Summer Palace, Fragrant Hills, and also Quanjude Roast Duck Restaurant. The restaurant has really become a place not to be missed when visiting Beijing.

It is a delightful experience watching the chef prepare the duck meat slices.

Although restaurants specialising in Peking roast duck abound in China, the most authentic Peking roast duck is still believed to be found only in Beijing itself.

It is believed by many that roast duck served by Quanjude is the most authentic. There are now many branches of the restaurant in Beijing. The one in the Qianmen area has a history of more than a hundred years.

Another restaurant called Bianyifang has a longer history than Quanjude in serving roast ducks. Bianyifang's roast ducks were even presented to the emperor in the Ming Dynasty. Quanjude broils the duck over a wood fire, while Bianyifang does it by putting the duck in a closed iron stove and broils the duck by heating the stove from the outside.

The broil stove has its origin in southern China. Before broiling the duck, the cook has to prepare firewood and ensure that the temperature of the stove is right. It is very difficult to broil ducks this way. If the temperature becomes too high, the ducks inside would be burnt. On the other hand, if the temperature gets too low, the ducks would not be properly cooked. This makes broiling the ducks over fire much easier, although stove-broiled ducks would certainly taste better. If the name of the restaurant has a "fang" in it, such as Bianyifang, it means that its roast ducks are stove-broiled.

Eating Peking roast duck is also a very unique experience. The chef will place the piping hot roast duck on a cart and prepare the dish in front of the customers. He does it so deftly that it looks somewhat like a performance. After serving the duck meat to the customers, the chef will use the bones to prepare a soup for the customers. Alternatively, customers can choose to take the bones home and use them to make soup.

When eating Peking roast duck, one wraps the duck skin and meat, along with slivers of spring onions and cucumber—dabbed with sweet sauce (*tian mian jiang*)—with a slice of thin pancake. This is the most authentic way to savour the rich flavour of the Peking roast duck.

LOCATION:
Quanjude Roast Duck Restaurant

32 Qianmen Dajie, Chongwen District.

PEKING UNIVERSITY

Peking University was founded in 1898. It was called Jingshi University at that time. It was both a comprehensive university and the government's education ministry. In 1912, it was renamed Peking University.

Cai Yuanpei, the famous educator and scholar, became the principal of Peking University in 1917. Cai believed in the freedom of thought. He was tolerant towards all kinds of scholars and ideas, and encouraged research in different fields. This helped to promote new systems of education in China. Peking University also laid a solid foundation for the New Cultural Movement and the May 4th Movement in the 1910s in Beijing.

Two famous scholars, Chen Duxiu and Li Dazhao, were invited to teach in Peking University in 1917. Chen Duxiu had started the *New Youth* magazine in Shanghai and initiated the New Cultural Movement. Following that, leaders of the movement would congregate at Peking University for the organisation of their activities.

Almost all of the best scholars in China were teaching in Peking University at that time. Cai Yuanpei tried to manage the university in a Western style. He succeeded in attracting distinguished scholars from various backgrounds. Scholars such as Liang Suming, Gu Hongming and Lin Yu believed that people should stick to traditional Chinese thinking while Chen Duxiu, Hu Shi, Lu Xun and Qian Xuantong believed that that change was what China needed in order to progress. These scholars taught in the same campus and debated in classrooms by giving speeches.

LOCATION:
5 Yiheyuanlu, Haidian District.

In 1918, there were 217 teachers in Peking University—90 of which were professors. There were 1,980 students—including 148 postgraduate students. It was the largest university in China then. Before the May 4th Movement in 1919, Peking University was the cradle of the New Cultural Movement.

At that time, Peking University was located in Mashen Temple of Jingshan East Street. Subsequently, it was relocated to Haidian District in the northwest of Beijing. Its former campus is now the office of the Ministry of Culture.

The present campus of Peking University at Zhongguancun in Haidian District occupies a much larger area than its former campus. New buildings of traditional Chinese style stand among green trees. The soul of Peking University is Weiminghu Lake, which is the finishing touch of this great university. Young students sit around the lake—to read or to simply relax. In an abstract way, it teaches them the meaning of life and the passage of time.

Peking University has in a sense bore witness to the era of change. It is now one of China's most prestigious universities and attracts students from all around the world.

Weiming Lake offers the students an idyllic place for relaxation.

QIANMEN

Qianmen (Qian Gate) is a symbol of old Beijing. Formally known as Zhengyangmen, Qianmen was the first of nine gates within the city of old Beijing. Qianmen or Daqianmen is a nickname given by the common people.

In the Qing Dynasty, operas were banned in the inner city. Many theatres were relocated outside to the streets in front of Qianmen. The area became a popular haunt for many Peking opera lovers who patronised the theatres there.

The beautifully renovated Qianmen Gate.

DISCOVER BEIJING

LOCATION:
Qianmen, Chongwen District.
You can get there by subway, getting off at Qianmen station.

Qianmen was made up of three sections: the watchtower, the archery tower and the enceinte. Inside the enceinte was a small square, which has two temples in it. In the event of an attack, soldiers would fire arrows at their enemies from the archery tower and hurl big logs at them from the top of the enceintes.

There used to be a bridge called Zhengyang Bridge over the moat outside Qianmen. Today, both the moat and the bridge are gone. What we see today in the area of Qianmen are just the remnants of a large group of buildings that had once seen better days.

QIANMEN **RAILWAY STATION**

An old building stands to the east of Qianmen. What we see now is a shopping complex. In fact, the building was an old railway station which had operated from the late Qing Dynasty till the 1950s. The station was built in 1901 and was called Qianmen Railway Station (Qianmen Huochezhan)—renamed from its former name, Zhengyangmen Railway Station.

In 1880, the government of the Qing Dynasty approved the request of Li Hongzhang, a high official of the time, to construct a railroad. In the following year, the railroad from Tangshan to Xugezhuang was constructed. In 1900, the Eight Allied Nations invaded China and divided the railroads of China among themselves. The British took over the section of the railway between Beijing to Shanhai Pass, and moved the station to Zhengyangmen (Zhengyang Gate).

Qianmen Railway Station is now a shopping complex.

LOCATION:

Near Qianmen, Chongwen District. You can get there by subway, getting off at Qianmen station.

DISCOVER BEIJING

By the time the Republic of China was founded, Qianmen Railway Station had become overcrowded. Between 1932 and 1934, more than 620,000 people took the train annually. Many people came to Beijing by train. For many first-time visitors to Beijing, the sight of Qianmen Railway Station was their first impression of the capital.

In the 1950s, a new station was built to the east of Qianmen Railway Station. Qianmen Railway Station then became the clubhouse for railway workers.

QIPAO

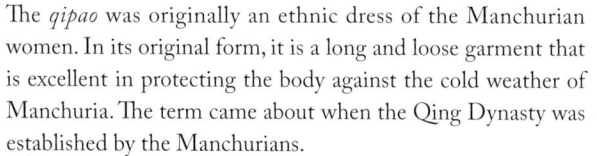

The modern-day qipao is a sexier version of its predecessor.

The *qipao* was originally an ethnic dress of the Manchurian women. In its original form, it is a long and loose garment that is excellent in protecting the body against the cold weather of Manchuria. The term came about when the Qing Dynasty was established by the Manchurians.

When the Manchurian rulers took over leadership in Beijing, they stationed their army—the Eight Banners—within the inner city of Beijing. The women of the Eight Banners—known also as Qiren (Banner People)—typically wore a one-piece dress (over a pair of pants) that came to be known as the *qipao* (Banner dress).

Although the Eight Banners comprised not only Manchurians, but also Mongolians and Han Chinese, the *qipao* was not worn by Han Chinese women who were not members of the Eight Banners. Instead, they wore a two-piece garment that comprised a blouse and a skirt.

Following the collapse of the Qing Dynasty, the *qipao* became a popular dress among the Chinese women as well, but not without first having variations made to it. This trend was the most apparent in the cosmopolitan city of Shanghai, which was the birthplace of the modern-day *qipao*.

In contrast to the loose-fitting *qipao* traditionally worn by the Manchurian women, the modified *qipao* is body-hugging and accentuates the figure. This modern version of the *qipao* soon took Shanghai by storm in the 1930s and 1940s and became a popular dress for women in high society.

The *qipao* can be worn for both formal and casual occasions. Elegant, sexy and stylishly charming, it remains a popular form of dress among Chinese women. In recent years, Western fashion designers have also adopted the design of the *qipao* in their works.

You can go to Ruifuxiang to have a beautiful *qipao* custom-made at:

1) 190 Wangfujing Dajie, Dongcheng District.

2) 5 Dashila Jie, Qianmenwai, Chongwen District.

DISCOVER BEIJING 105

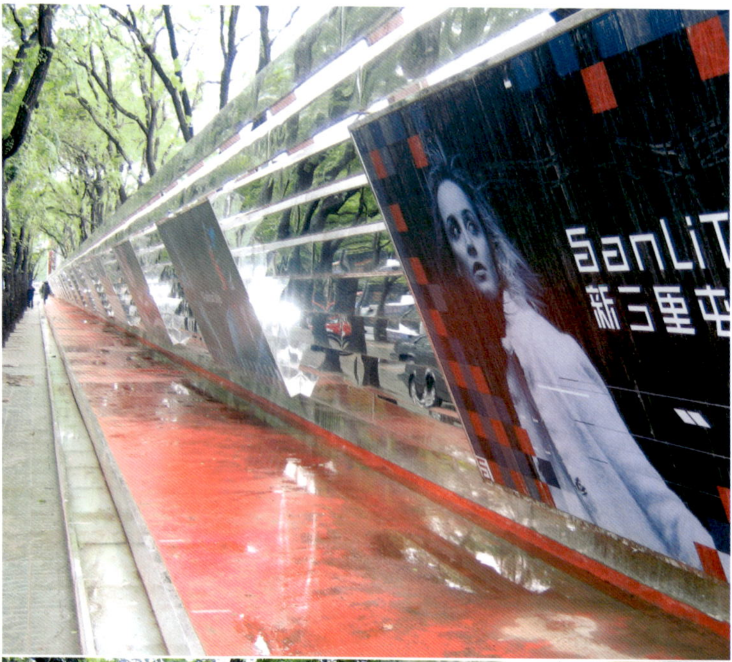

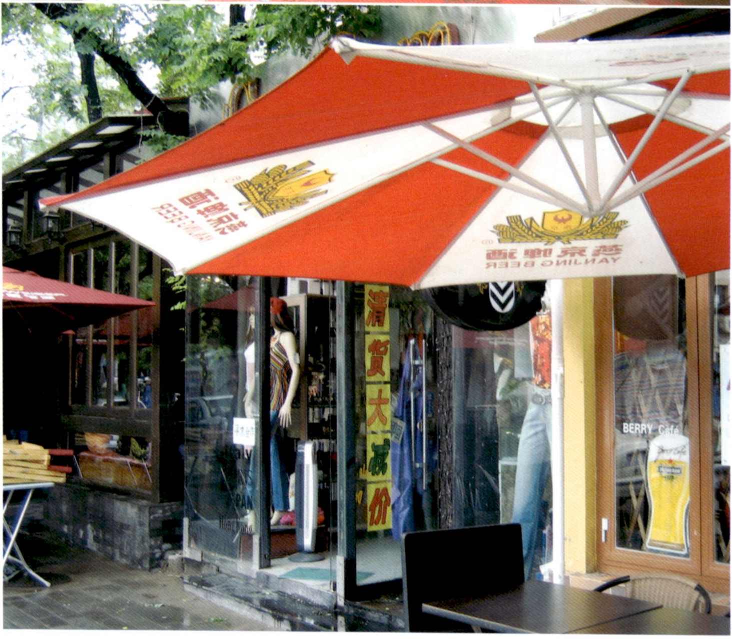
燕京啤酒
YANJING BEER
清货大减价
BERRY Café

SANLITUN

Sanlitun is a favourite haunt of many locals and foreigners in Beijing.

Sanlitun, an area located to the west of Changhong Bridge on the West 3rd Ring Road and next to the embassy area, is popular because of the pubs that line the streets. Embracing a combination of Chinese culture and Western culture, Sanlitun is a favourite hangout for the foreigners. Every evening, many foreigners would flock to the pubs there to savour the unique East-West flavour of this street.

Sanlitun is a new window of Beijing. Pubs on the street open from noon till dawn of the following day. Almost all the visitors from abroad have heard of this place and many would not give it a miss when they visit Beijing. Perhaps what Sanlitun means to them is just like what Chinatown in Western countries represent to the Chinese people.

Sanlitun has been a famous night haunt for almost 10 years. Other than the pubs, businesses such as boutiques and auto repair workshops flourish too. Now its customers mainly fall into three categories: foreigners, white-collar workers and people who work in the media, culture and entertainment industries.

Though there are some places in Beijing which are better than Sanlitun in terms of architecture and layout, Sanlitun remains as one of the busiest and most popular places.

Some problems have also arisen as its businesses develop. Noise from the pubs and crowds has caused disturbance to the residents in the neighbourhood, some buildings and trees have been taken down to make room for the pubs, and plumbing and electrical infrastructure require frequent servicing.

In view of these problems, some people have suggested that the pubs should be relocated out of Sanlitun. However, the proposal has not been accepted by the authorities. The pubs there continue to be enjoyed by its regular patrons and foreign visitors.

LOCATION:
Sanlitun Jiuba Jie, west of Changhongqiao, Chaoyang District.

SHEJITAN (Zhongshan Park)

In the past, only the emperors and the imperial family were allowed entry to the five altars and eight temples in Beijing. Shejitan was one of these consecrated places that glowed with the majestic aura of the imperial family and drew endless interest from the commoners.

The five altars are Tiantan (Altar of Heaven), Ditan (Altar of Earth), Ritan (Altar of the Sun), Yuetan (Altar of the Moon) and Shejitan (Altar of Land and Grain).

The eight temples are Taimiao (Ancestral Temple), Fengxian Temple, Chuanxin Temple, Shouhuang Temple, Tangzi Temple, Emperors Temple, Yonghegong Lama Temple and Confucius Temple.

Visits to the temples and altars were solely for the purpose of conducting regular religious rituals.

It was not until 10th October 1914 that Shejitan raised its mysterious veil. Led by Duan Qirui, the local governor, people from all walks of life donated money to rebuild Shejitan into a park for the new era. Renamed Zhongyang Park, Shejitan was open to the public.

Shejitan symbolised the God of Land and Grain. One Chinese ancient classic refers to '*She*' as 'the superior of all land', while *Ji* refers to "the elder of all grains". Grains grow on land, so '*She*' and '*Ji*' can never be separated. As people believed that they were created out of earth and that the land provided them with food, they worshipped the God of Land and Grain as the creator and protector of human beings. Both emperors and commoners were equally protected by the God of Land and Grain.

Shejitan was built in a typical Chinese ancient monarchal style. There was no entrance in the south, north and west, but there were three gates in the east that were entrances meant for the imperial family and watchmen. After Shejitan was converted into a park, another gate was constructed at the south wall along Chang'an Street (to the west of Tian'anmen).

Later, Zhongyang Park was renamed Zhongshan Park to commemorate Dr Sun Yat-sen. Although it is situated in the centre of the downtown area, the park exudes a sense of tranquility with fences separating this peaceful park from the hustle and bustle of the crowds.

LOCATION:

Northwest of Tian'anmen Square.

You can get there by subway, getting off at Tian'anmenxi station.

After Shejitan became a park, several teahouses were set up in it and business was extremely good. Three teahouses, Chun Ming Teahouse, Chang Mei Teahouse and Bo Si Xing Teahouse, became the busiest establishments in the park.

Springtime in Zhongshan Park.

SHICHAHAI

Shichahai is the city's lake district that combines both modern and ancient elements. Here, well-preserved princes' mansions, *hutong* (lanes) and bridges form one of the most beautiful sceneries of Beijing. The traditional Beijing *hutong* culture blends with popular modern culture—creating an amazing new look to Shichahai.

Shichahai comprises three lakes—Qianhai, Houhai and Jishuitan—presenting to visitors an idyllic sight of rippling lakes surrounded by weeping willows.

There are several interpretations of the origin of its name. One version is that there were 10 ancient temples (*cha* means 'temple' in Chinese) in the lake district; another version is that since the Ming Dynasty, the water level in Shichahai has gone down, so

The lanes in Shichahai are dotted with restaurants and shops.

there are both water surfaces and land in the lakes. In Buddhism, field or land is called "*cha*", and people in Beijing usually refer to a big area of water as "*hai*" (sea). "*Shi*" (ten) denotes a great number. In addition to these two versions, some people say that once there was a famous stone floodgate, so the lake district was called "Shizhahai (Stone Floodgate Lake)". And it was changed to " Shichahai" by a slip of the tongue.

Only one ancient temple—Guanghua Temple—was preserved along the banks of Shichahai. It is enjoyable to sit along the banks of Shichahai with a cup of tea, looking out at the lake and listening to the toll of the bell from the temple.

Yinding Bridge is as famous as Shichahai. It is located at the part where Qianhai connects with Houhai. Standing on the bridge, one can see Houhai at the north where the water and the sky merge as one. The bridge and the water that flows beneath

Yinding Bridge at Shichahai.

it certainly make a charming view. The west of Yinding Bridge is Houhai—the west of which is Jishuitan. Huitong Temple is at the northwest island.

In the Yuan Dynasty, ships would sail along the Jinghang Grand Canal and arrive at Jishuitan by travelling along Tonghui River. After the Ming Dynasty, Jishuitan was disconnected from the canal and became a lake.

Now, after several improvements, Shichahai has become an ideal place for people to row boats in and swim during summer, and skate in winter. On ordinary days, people would stroll beside the lake, walking their dogs. It is indeed a relaxing experience walking around the lake, taking in the sights and scents of the lotuses, which are in full bloom in spring.

Dining at the restaurants along Shichahai may be an expensive experience for many local Beijingers. However, these restaurants are mainly popular with foreign tourists, who find it a delightful experience dining by the lake, especially in the evenings.

Other than the popular Chinese restaurants such as Kongyiji Restaurant, Zhuzhiyuan Restaurant and Chan Teahouse, Shichahai also offers a variety of shops, cafés and pubs that are popular with the locals and foreign visitors.

Dining by the lake at Shichahai as night falls.

LOCATION:
Xicheng District.

SNACKS

Beijing snacks—which combine varied flavours from different Chinese ethnic groups like Han, Hui, Meng, Man and imperial snacks from the Ming Dynasty (1368–1644) and the Qing Dynasty (1644–1911)—come in many varieties and have their own characteristics.

There are over 200 kinds of snacks in Beijing, including dishes to go with wine, such as fried tripe (Bao Du) and boiled sheep's head (Bai Shui Yang Tou); pastry desserts like pancakes with meat-fillings (Rou Mo Shao Bing) and other snacks for breakfast or supper, like sticky rice with sweet fillings (Ai Wo Wo) and "rolling donkey" (Lu Da Gun), a steamed rice cake filled with red bean paste. Fermented drink made from ground beans (Dou Zhi), fried liver (Chao Gan) and filled sausage (Guan Chang) are especially popular with the older Beijingers.

In Beijing, there are also several places that are known for their snacks, such as the Donghuamen, Longfusi Temple and Wangfujing. Today, the number of authentic snacks that can be found in Beijing has decreased tremendously but there are still some snacks that have withstood the test of time.

The following are some popular snacks that can be found in Beijing.

Fried Liver

Fried liver is a unique snack in Beijing. It is made from mashed livers and intestines of pigs and boiled with various seasonings and starch. The most authentic fried liver can only be found in time-honoured shops. There is one shop near Qianmen that is well known for its fried liver. Hailed as having the best fried liver in Beijing, it attracts large crowds every day.

Fermented Juice

Fermented juice is a thick fermented drink made from ground beans. It has a musty smell and sour taste. Known to be extremely popular in Beijing during the Qing Dynasty, it is still regarded as the tastiest drink by many Beijingers. Closely related to this fermented drink is the "pockmarked beancurd", which is made from bean dregs. It is usually served with pepper oil or fried salted mustard.

Rice Flour Cake

In making rice flour cake, a dough made from rice flour is steamed and spread on a smooth board. It is then topped with brown sugar and sweetened bean paste and rolled with fried noodles. It can be enjoyed with the juice of sweet-scented osmanthus.

Ai Wo Wo

Ai Wo Wo is a traditional snack of the Hui ethnic minority. It is a steamed cone-shaped cake made of glutinous rice or millet with sweet filling. It first appeared in the Yuan Dynasty and was popular with the imperial family during the Ming and Qing dynasties. It melts easily in the mouth and is an ideal dish to savour in summer. Now it is one of the snacks popular with many Beijingers.

Corn Flour Cake

In making corn flour cakes, fine corn flour is first selected and sifted. Then fine bean paste is mixed with the corn flour, which is then steamed with sweet-scented osmanthus and white sugar.

Sheep-eye Steamed Bun

Sheep-eye steamed bun was a snack fancied by Emperor Kangxi. Its name is derived from its shape, which looks like a sheep's eye. Though small in size, sheep-eye steamed buns are widely popular, thanks to a wide range of ingredients that can be used as a filling.

Beijingers queuing up for delicious local snacks.

LOCATION:

Taste various snacks at Longfusi snack bars, Dongsi Dajie or Huguosi snack bar, Huguosi Dajie, Xicheng District.

There are also all kinds of delicious snacks at Donghuamen night market, north of Wangfujing.

DISCOVER BEIJING 115

TAIMIAO
(Cultural Palace of the Working People)

Taimiao, or the Ancestral Temple was the imperial family's temple and the home of their ancestors' memorial tablets.

Taimiao was where the domestic affairs of the emperors took place. From enthronement to marriage, to the births of their children, setting off for battles and celebrating their victory in battles, the emperors would offer sacrifices to their ancestors at Taimiao. These were significant occasions where the emperors

Crowds throng the Cultural Palace of Working People everyday.

gave thanks to their ancestors for their blessings, as well as sought protection for their endeavours.

In Chinese society, ancestor worship plays an important role in people's lives. On the first day of every season, people would offer sacrifices to their ancestors. Taimiao, which was different from the ancestral temples of the common people, had certain unique features. The ritual hall was divided into several sacrificial rooms. Within each room were imperials seats that were used as altars of the dead emperor and his empresses. The emperor's imperial seat was flanked on both sides by the imperial seats of his empresses. This showed that even in death the emperors needed their own private space. Each deceased emperor had his own room, which was very spacious.

The wish for a long reign was common to every emperor. Alas, it remained just that. The Qing Dynasty finally came to an end as the last emperor Puyi was driven out of the Forbidden City. Taimiao became a desolate place as the final chapter that recorded the last years of the feudal society drew to a close.

Just as Shejitan has become a public park, Taimiao is now the Cultural Palace of Working People. Zhongshan Park is situated west of Tian'anmen, while the Cultural Palace of Working People is located east of Tian'anmen. When it became the Cultural Palace of Working People, the former inscribed board of Taimiao was removed and placed in the sacrificial hall for several decades. Now, this inscribed board is hung on the western gate of the Forbidden City. This is purely for tourists visiting Taimiao. After all, Taimiao was an indispensable part of the entire structure of the Forbidden City.

LOCATION:

Northeast of Tian'anmen Square, Dongcheng District.

You can get there by subway, getting off at Tian'anmendong station.

TAORANTING PARK

A reminder of the men of letters who found their resting place at Taoranting Park.

Many people visit Taoranting Park not only for its beautiful scenery but also for the tombs at the northern section of the park. There are many tombs inside Taoranting Park. These are the tombs of celebrities as well as the common people. There is a sad story behind almost every gravestone.

On a mound in the west of the Taoranting Park, there is a tomb of the legendary courtesan, Du Shiniang, of the Qing Dynasty. The inscriptions on the tombstone tell the story of how Du Shiniang had selflessly saved the life of her lover. Unfortunately, it has now been proven that this tomb of Du Shiniang is a fake. However it is true that Saijinhua, the famous courtesan of the late Qing Dynasty, was once buried in Taoranting Park.

There is also a public cemetery for Peking opera actors at Taoranting Park. The plot of land was purchased by Cheng Changgeng (a famous opera actor of the Qing Dynasty) and other opera actors in 1871. The location of one's burial ground meant a lot to the common people at that time. Every family had its own burial ground. Family members who had committed serious crimes or engaged in professions such as acting in operas were forbidden to be buried in the family burial ground. Therefore, the burial ground in Taoranting Park was specifically for these opera actors.

LOCATION:
19 Taiping Jie, Xuanwu District.
You can get there by subway, the nearest station is Xuanwumen.

TEAHOUSES

There are teahouses all over China. Tea culture is a legacy of China's thousands of years of history. The tea culture of China can roughly be divided into *Chadao* (a special tea ceremony popular among government officials and intellectuals) and the culture of the teahouses.

The Traditional *Chadao* is too meticulous and abstract for the common people. People sip tea from a tiny cup and call it "tea appreciation" instead of "tea drinking". The culture of teahouses in old Beijing was just the opposite. The teahouses were noisy and jolly. This was because of the sociable nature of the Beijingers. They loved chatting with friends and teahouses provided them with the best venue to do so.

In the 1910s and 1920s, there were teahouses on every street in Beijing. They were like the cafés of Paris. Lao She, a famous novelist, was very interested in what took place in teahouses. Based on his observation and study of the character of the customers of the teahouses and the topics they discussed, Lao She wrote a play called *The Teahouse*. Fifty years later, the play is still being performed.

There were many kinds of teahouses in the late Qing Dynasty. The most expensive ones are called "Qing (Clear) teahouses". Young people from wealthy families would rest at these teahouses in the morning after their morning strolls with their prized pet birds. On the ceiling of the teahouse were hooks for them to hang their birdcages. Businessmen also liked to visit these teahouses at noon to negotiate business deals.

Other kinds of teahouses include "Story teahouses" where customers could listen to artistes telling classical stories and "Chess teahouses" where customers play Chinese chess while drinking tea. Alcohol was also served at certain teahouses. Everyone could find a teahouse that best suited his interest.

In the Qing Dynasty, the city of Beijing was dotted with teahouses. Even in the remotest corners or alleys, people could find some tiny teahouses. In the first half of the 20th century when China was in chaos from internal wars, few people had the time or the money to patronise teahouses. Because of this, many teahouses went out of business.

Lao She Teahouse—inspired by the teahouses that populated Beijing in the past.

DISCOVER BEIJING | 121

In 1949, following the establishment of the People's Republic of China, there were only a few teahouses left in Beijing. Lao She Teahouse, the most famous teahouse in Beijing today, was founded in 1988. Five Happiness Teahouse was opened near Di'anmen in 1994. After that, thousands of teahouses sprang up across Beijing in the next 10 years.

In the 1930s, the teahouses inside Zhongshan Park were very popular. Of the five or six teahouses in Zhongshan Park, Chunming Teahouse, Changmei Teahouse and Baisixin Teahouse were the most popular ones. Many old Beijingers still remember their names.

The teahouses in Sichuan and Yunnan Provinces are also good places to visit. The teahouses in the south are slightly different from those in the north. Teahouses in Beijing reflect the way of life in this city and the characteristics of the people here. It seems Beijingers are the most talkative and humorous among all the Chinese people. They also like to discuss politics. The teahouses are places for them to show their oratorical skills and they are not very particular about the tea, although most Beijingers like scented tea. This love of scented tea would surprise most southerners, who prefer green tea and who believe that scented tea is not fresh.

LOCATION:
3rd Building, Zhengyang Market, Qianmenxi Dajie, Xuanwu District.

The nearest subway station is Qianmen.

Another view of Lao She Teahouse.

THE BELL AND DRUM TOWERS (Zhonggulou)

The Bell Tower. The Bell and Drum Towers (Zhonggulou) were built in 1272 during the Yuan Dynasty. They were called Qizheng Towers at the time. The function of the towers—by beating the drum and tolling the bell—was to tell time.

The main chronometer of the two towers was a bronze water clock. The water clock consisted of several bronze pots with scales of time carved on the sides of the pots. The pots were placed one above another to enable water to drip slowly from one pot to another. Intricate mechanism ensured that when the water ran out in one pot, a pair of gongs would be struck. At the same time, 24 drums were beaten to announce the time.

The water clock was originally made in the Song Dynasty. When the Mongolians occupied China, it was moved from Kaifeng (the capital of the Song Dynasty) to Beijing.

The Bell Tower and Drum Tower were built along the central axis of Beijing city. The Chinese attach great importance to symmetry and the central location. The central axis was an imaginary line that cut across the centre of Beijing in a north-

The Drum Tower.

DISCOVER BEIJING 125

LOCATION:
Di'anmen Dajie, Dongcheng District. You can get there by subway. The nearest station is Guloudajie.

south direction. Most of the important buildings in the city were built on this line. This central axis starts from Zhengyangmen in the south, through the Forbidden City and to the Drum Tower in the north. The Bell Tower is located north of the Drum Tower. There is still one big drum left in the Drum Tower. The rest of the drums were destroyed by the Eight Allied Nation troops (Baguolianjun) in 1900.

THE **FORBIDDEN CITY**

The Forbidden City (Gugong Museum) was the Chinese imperial palace built in 1420. It is probably one of the most famous ancient palaces in the world. The principles applied in designing this palace are balance and symmetry. The Chinese believe that the sky is round while the earth is square. Both palaces and local residences such as the courtyard houses are surrounded by square yards. For the Forbidden City, the main halls are built along a central axis. Secondary rooms are usually located symmetrically on both sides of the main halls.

Taihe Hall was the venue for the Emperor's most important ceremonies, such as his birthday.

DISCOVER BEIJING

According to ancient Chinese astrology, the Polaris or North Star (*Zi Wei Geng*) is at the centre of the universe and it is where the heavenly emperor resides. Hence the name "*Zi Jin Cheng*"—the Forbidden City—the palace meant only for the emperors on earth.

The Imperial Passageway along the central axis of the Forbidden City was meant for the imperial carriage or sedan chair and was for the emperor's exclusive use. Officials and eunuchs could only walk on the steps at the sides. The same rules applied to the gates of Forbidden City—only the emperor could walk through Tian'anmen, the Gate of Heavenly Peace.

A huge stone was inlaid on the Imperial Passageway north of Taihe Hall. The stone is 16.57 metres long, 3.07 metres wide and 1.7 metres thick—the largest existing stone carving in China. Patterns of dragons were carved on the stone. The Chinese believed that the heavy stone would, metaphorically, hold the palace firmly in place to prevent it from being "blown away by the wind".

In front of Taihe Hall, there are a marble sundial, a marble measuring barrel, a bronze crane and a bronze tortoise. In China, both the crane and the tortoise are symbols of everlasting rule and longevity.

In front of each of the three main halls of the Forbidden City is a pair of enormous bronze vats that used to store water for putting out fires, a frequent occurrence in the palace. Over 20 serious cases of fires—caused by lightning, lit candles and burning incense—were recorded.

These vats were called "lucky vats". They were also known as "the sea at the door" (*men hai*). In winter, when the temperature dropped, there were special covers for the vats. Each cover had a depression in the centre for charcoal. This prevented the water from freezing. There are altogether 308 lucky vats in the Forbidden City. Apart from the vats, there are also about 80 wells inside the Forbidden City. Water from these wells, as well as the city moat, was also used to put out fires.

It is said that the overall arrangement of the halls and rooms in the Forbidden City was based strictly on horoscopes. Every room has a matching position with a particular star in the sky. Therefore, the 9,999 rooms in the Forbidden City would symbolise 9,999 stars. The emperor himself would be the 10,000th star—above all the stars in the universe.

However, it is interesting to note that the definition of a room in the Forbidden City is unlike what it generally refers to. In the Forbidden City, even the square spaces between the columns are also counted as rooms. For instance, the largest hall, Taihe Hall, is counted as 55 rooms. In actual fact, there are a total of 980 rooms in the Forbidden City.

Puyi, the last emperor of the Qing Dynasty, was forced to abdicate in 1912. However, he was allowed to live in the Forbidden City until 1924 before he was finally driven out of it. From that day on, the Forbidden City was no longer for the exclusive use of the emperors of China. Anyone can visit the Forbidden City as long as he buys an admission ticket.

The Forbidden City is like a palace of dragons. Dragons were symbols of emperors in China for thousands of years. Only the emperors could use dragons as motifs on the items they used. Visitors to the Forbidden City today can see dragon motifs carved or painted on almost every item in the palace. In the past, any person caught using dragon motifs on clothing and ornaments would be beheaded as it was considered a serious offence to impersonate the emperor.

There are also some sad stories that took place within the Forbidden City. Probably the most tragic story is that of Emperor Guangxu and his favourite wife, Zhenfei.

Although Guangxu was the emperor, it was the Empress Dowager Cixi who was in power. Both of them had become bitter enemies in their struggle for power. As Zhenfei had somewhat taken on the role of an advisor to Emperor Guangxu, she antagonised Cixi as well.

After Emperor Guangxu suffered a defeat in the political reform of 1898, Cixi held him prisoner in Yingtai Isle and placed Zhenfei under house arrest in the palace. During the Boxer Rebellion, when Cixi was fleeing to Xi'an, she ordered Zhenfei to be drowned in a well in the Forbidden City. Guangxu was forced to follow Cixi to Xi'an, without having a final look at his beloved wife.

Cixi probably never imagined that she would immortalise Zhenfei. The small well where Zhenfei was drowned is now called Zhenfei Well, and is a main attraction for visitors to the Forbidden City today.

LOCATION:

Chang'an Avenue, Dongcheng District.

You can get there by subway. The nearest stations are Tian'anmen East and Tian'anmen West.

THE GREAT WALL

Qin Shihuang, the first emperor of China, was the first Chinese ruler who initiated the massive construction project of linking up the walls built respectively by the kingdoms of Qin, Yan and Zhao. As a whole, the Great Wall runs from Lintao in the west and winds its way to Xiangping in the east. The centre of it is in Beijing.

Today, the Great Wall is a UNESCO World Heritage Site. The three sections of the Great Wall that visitors can make a trip to from Beijing are Badaling, Simatai and Mutianyu.

The Great Wall at Badaling in Yanqing County was famous for its peculiar shape and strategic location. This part of the Great

DISCOVER BEIJING

Wall is 3,741 metres long. It runs atop the range of mountains and resembles a huge dragon.

Juyong Pass on Badaling Great Wall was built in 1505 during the Ming Dynasty. It has two gates that were made of stone and brick. On top of the gates are platforms that are connected to the walls on both sides. These platforms were used as observation posts, for the posting of sentries and storing of weapons.

Mao Zedong's saying, "He who has not climbed the Great Wall is not a real man", was originally used in boosting the morale of his troops during the revolution. It is now a promotional phrase for the Great Wall. This saying is engraved on a stone tablet atop the highest point at Badaling Great Wall. Called the "Real Man Slope", the section is 888 metres above sea level.

The Mutianyu section of the Great Wall is connected to Juyong Pass in the west and Gubeikou Gateway in the east. One of the best-preserved sections of the Great Wall, Mutianyu stands out for its unique design.

In the Ming Dynasty, as many battles took place at Mutianyu Great Wall, this section was reconstructed with additional beacon towers (22 in all), which provided more storage space for weapons. The defence function of this section was further enhanced with both the outer and inner parapets crenellated, allowing shots to be fired at enemy troops on both sides.

Mutianyu Pass was built in a valley and was formed by three beacon towers connected to one another via their interior, with the one in the middle taller and wider than the two at the sides. This structure is rare among all the sections of the Great Wall.

Simatai Great Wall is considered by many visitors to be the most beautiful yet most hazardous section of the Great Wall. It measures 5.4 kilometres in length and features a total of 35 beacon towers. Located at Gubeikou of Miyun County—about 130 kilometres from the city of Beijing—it is the most authentic and rugged section as no restoration work has been done on it.

Simatai Great Wall boasts a number of amazing scenic spots. At Wangjinglou ("Viewing Beijing Tower"), situated at an elevation of 986 metres, one can see Beijing in the distance, especially in the night. There is also the "Stairway to Heaven" (Tian Ti)—a steep section at an incline of almost 90 degrees that leads to Wangjinglou.

LOCATION:

Badaling Great Wall: Yanqin County.

Juyongguan Great Wall: South of Badaling.

Mutianyu Great Wall: Mutianyu Town, Huairou District.

Simatai Great Wall: Gubeikou, Miyun County.

A view of the Great Wall in winter.

THE IMPERIAL ARCHIVE

The Imperial Archive (Huangshicheng) is located to the southwest of the Forbidden City. It was built in 1536 and was named Shenyuge—later renamed as Huangshicheng.

The Imperial Archive was for the storage of imperial edicts, files, and the emperors' records. It also stored books, such as the *Yongle Encyclopedia* (China's first encyclopedia), *The Compendia of Qing Law*, and the imperial genealogy record. It was renovated twice in 1568 and in 1807. After 460 years, it is perfectly preserved but is now disused.

In the olden days, timber was commonly used in building a house. For fear of fire, Huangshicheng was built entirely with stones. Not one single piece of wood was used. Surrounded by red walls, its main hall was built on a 2-metre stone base and rounded by white marble rails. Its roof was covered with yellow glazed tiles. The doors and windows were all made of white marble.

Inside the main hall there are 152 book cabinets—made of camphor wood covered with copper sheets. There are many windows in the wall and the whole hall is cool and dry. Since no lumber is used in the building of the hall, it is also fireproof.

As early as the Qin Dynasty and the Han Dynasty, emperors ordered stone houses to be built for storing imperial files and edicts. From then on, many imperial archives have been built. The Imperial Archive—of the Ming and Qing dynasties—is the only one that has survived.

The Imperial Archive—as it was in the past.

One of the stadiums where the Olympic Games will be held.

THE OLYMPIC VILLAGE

New maps of Beijing will show the Olympic Village for the 2008 Olympic Games. Yet it is hard to discuss its history as changes occur every day.

The Olympic Village is located near the crossroad of Zhongzhou Road and the 4th Ring Road. It starts from the former Olympic Centre and stretches northward. To the north of the Olympic Village is Xindian Road, and to the south, the World Trade Centre and the Institute of Geographic Sciences and Natural Resources Research of the Chinese Academy of Science. Beichendong Street and Baimiaocun Street are on the east and west side of the Olympic Village.

This area used to be a piece of vacant land. Due to the dry weather and poor soil quality, it was not suitable for agricultural use. It is also a considerable distance away from the Forbidden City and the other 25 Historical and Cultural Communities of Beijing. Therefore the development of modern buildings and architecture in this area would hardly affect the landscape of old Beijing. To the west of the Olympic Village is the Zhongguancun Hi-tech Park where many hi-tech enterprises are situated. To the east is the Central Business District of Beijing. The Olympic Village will connect these two areas.

Thirty-seven stadiums are required for the 2008 Olympic Games. Thirty-two of these stadiums are in Beijing and 19 of them are new. After the Olympic Games, these stadiums will

One of the stadiums where the 2008 Olympic Games will be held.

either become facilities for public entertainment or training bases for professional sportsmen and venues for matches and tournaments. Many of these stadiums are designed with commercial facilities. A few of the stadiums are temporary and will be dismantled after the Olympic Games. The rest are permanent structures such as the Olympic Park and Wukesong Sports Centre.

The Beijing National Stadium will be hosting the finals of the gymnastics, handball and volleyball events during the 2008 Olympic Games. After that, it will be used for major entertainment events. The National Swimming Centre will become a water leisure park after 2008.

Some stadiums to be built in the next few years will be used for table tennis, badminton, fencing and wrestling, or as news centres and broadcasting centres. After the Olympic Games, they will be used as cultural facilities or exhibition venues.

The 11th Asian Games was held in Beijing in 1990. The National Olympic Sports Centre and the Asian Games Village were built in preparation for it together with an international conference centre, hotels and museums. It helped boost the development of the northern part of Beijing. Now the Asian Games Village area has become the most attractive community of Beijing. One can imagine the future of the Olympic Village after 2008.

THE TEMPLE OF THE
RECLINING BUDDHA (Wofosi)

At the foot of Fragrant Hills (Xiangshan) is a famous temple —the Temple of the Reclining Buddha (Wofosi)—with a history of more than 1,000 years. It was built in 628 during the Tang Dynasty. The famous statue of the reclining Buddha in the temple is 5.3 metres long and 1.6 metres high. It was cast in bronze in 1321 during the Yuan Dynasty and weighs around 5.4 tons—the largest of its kind in China.

In the compound of the temple were originally three sala trees. Sala trees are sacred to Buddhists. (Long ago, two sala trees had sheltered the Buddha Sakyamuni from the scorching sun while

One of the prayer halls at the Temple of the Reclining Buddha.

he meditated.) Now there is only one sala tree in front of the Hall of the Three Buddhas (Sanshi Fodian). It was planted in 1954 to replace the original tree, which was uprooted by strong winds during a violent storm on 4 May 1949.

The Temple of the Reclining Buddha is not the original name of the temple. In the Tang Dynasty, it was called Doushuai Temple; in the Yuan Dynasty, Zhaohong Temple and subsequently, Hongqing Temple. In 1443 of the Ming Dynasty, it was called Anqichan Temple and later, Yong'an Temple. Its last known official name was Shifang Pujue Temple, given by Emperor Yongzheng (reign 1722–1735) of the Qing Dynasty. The name Wofosi was actually popularised by the general public as the statue of the reclining Buddha is the most distinctive feature of the temple.

During the Ming Dynasty, five emperors donated money to renovate the temple. Emperor Yingzong of the Ming Dynasty (reign 1436–1450 and 1457–1464) also donated a set of Tibetan Buddhist sutra. And Emperor Xianzong (reign 1465–1487) had a stupa built in the temple compound.

Emperors of the Qing Dynasty made even more frequent visits to the Temple of the Reclining Buddha. Emperor Qianlong was fond of the place and he even had a statue of himself installed in the temple.

The Temple of the Reclining Buddha is now made up of seven halls—all facing the south—parallel to one another in three groups. On both sides of the temple are three courtyard houses linked by covered walkways. These houses were a summer retreat for the emperor. To the east of the temple is another group of courtyard houses that were the dormitory of the monks. The overall architectural style of the temple is characterised by balance and symmetry. According to the influential Chinese architect, Liang Sicheng, this is a classic example of the seven-hall architectural style prevalent in the Tang and Song dynasties.

LOCATION:

Beijing Botanical Gardens.

Near Fragrant Hills (Xiang Shan), Haidian District.

TIAN'ANMEN SQUARE

In 1420, the Ming Dynasty completed the construction of city walls, imperial palaces, temples, official buildings and residential housing in Beijing as part of the plan to prepare for its transfer of the capital city from the south. This means that Tian'anmen Square—in its very original shape—came into being during this time.

The square is located between Tian'anmen (Gate of Heavenly Peace) and Qianmen (Qian Gate). Its size today is the result of several expansions over a long period of time. There is also a Russian element in the layout of the Tian'anmen Square, which was an adoption of the designs of the Kremlin Palace and the Red Square by the former Soviet Union advisors following the founding of the People's Republic of China in 1949. The government buildings were built with Tian'anmen as the centre, the square in front of Tian'anmen was greatly expanded for public gathering and demonstration, and in the middle of Tian'anmen Square was the Monument to the People's Heroes.

To the west of the Square is the Great Hall of the People and to the east is the Museum of the Chinese Revolution. In 1976, upon the death of Mao Zedong, the Memorial Hall of Chairman Mao was built next to the Monument to the People's Heroes in the south of the Square. In the Hall is the body of the leader kept in a crystal coffin and open to viewing by visitors from all over the world.

For more than half a century, the red five-star national flag of China has been raised in Tian'anmen Square every morning. During the visit of distinguished state guests, red carpets would be rolled out at a corner of the square and the guards of honour would be reviewed.

Tian'anmen Square and the surrounding vistas knit together more than 500 years of China's history. Spatially, Tian'anmen Square is both an epitome of China and a window for the world to gain a glimpse of the country.

Particularly, many of the momentous events occurring at Tian'anmen Square in the 20th century have become either the turning point or watershed in modern Chinese history. And most of the movements and revolutions that took place at Tian'anmen Square succeeded in achieving their goals.

On 4 May 1919, more than 3,000 students gathered at Tian'anmen Square, calling for the government not to ratify and sign the Versailles Treaty. This protest sparked off the May 4th Movement, which saw a nationwide anti-feudalism and anti-imperialism struggle and also marked the beginning of China's new-democratic revolution.

On 9 December 1935, the December 9th Movement that took place at Tian'anmen Square sparked off a massive national protest of the Japanese invasion that broke out in 1937.

On 1 October 1949, Chairman Mao Zedong solemnly declared to the masses and soldiers at Tian'anmen Square: "The Central Government of the People's Republic of China has been founded today!" From that year onwards, Tian'anmen Square sees the grand celebrations on each and every National Day.

On 18 August 1966, Chairman Mao met with the Red Guards on the rostrum of Tian'anmen and shook hands with the masses down at Tian'anmen Square, which, at that time, saw the large gathering of the Red Guards. This marked the end of the Cultural Revolution, which had plunged the country into a decade-long period of chaos and upheavals.

On 5 April 1976, the death of Premier Zhou Enlai triggered the Tian'anmen Event, or the April 5th Movement, at Tian'anmen Square. The square was then filled with wreaths and elegiac couplets. Popular sentiments at that time soon brought the downfall of the Gang of Four—Yao Wenyuan, Jiang Qing, Zhang Chunqiao and Wang Hongwen—four radical figures

The portrait of Mao Zedong overlooking Tian'anmen Square.

who played a dominant political role during the later period of the Cultural Revolution.

All these events—among others—that took place at Tian'anmen Square seem to illustrate another rarely recognised character of squares: memories of a square are an alternative text to recorded history of a city.

In 20th century China, Tian'anmen Square witnessed its entire transformation from a period of slumber to an awakening. Tian'anmen, from which the square derived its name and against which the square stands in such charming contrast, used to be the principal front of the imperial palace of both the Ming and Qing dynasties.

Jinshui River, Jinshui Bridge, the two pairs of stone lions, as well as the two colossal ornamental columns in front of Tian'anmen are full of totem significance in Chinese culture and a symbol of China's 5,000 years of history.

In January 1988, the rostrum of Tian'anmen Gate was open to visitors from home and abroad. Now we can take in the view of Tian'anmen Square from the rostrum of Tian'anmen.

LOCATION:
Tian'anmen Square, Dongcheng District.

TIANTAN (The Altar of Heaven)

Tiantan (the Altar of Heaven) reflects the Chinese belief of the causational relationship between weather and harvesting.

Praying for good weather is a custom among the Chinese people. The ancient Chinese believed that Heaven was an almighty god that controlled everything under the sky. Survival was dependent on Heaven's will. Hence, people believe in Heaven wholeheartedly and unconditionally. The architecture of Tiantan is solemn and stately. It is the temple of all temples. To the Chinese people, Heaven is an omnipresent god of nature and is the highest god in the universe.

During the reign of the Ming emperor Yongle, Tiantan was built outside Zhengyangmen to show that the imperial court attached great importance to agriculture. It became the venue where the emperors held prayers to Heaven for blessings of good harvests.

During Emperor Jiajing's reign, Beijing was invaded by the Mongolians. To prevent Tiantan from being destroyed by the Mongolians, a city was built around it as a security measure. This shows the importance of Tiantan to the Chinese. Sacrificial ceremonies revering Heaven were also the most solemn of all religious rituals in ancient China.

The Hall of Prayer for Good Harvest at Tiantan.

DISCOVER BEIJING 143

The Echo Wall at Tiantan.

In Beijing, Tiantan is the only building that can be compared with the Forbidden City in terms of its splendour. This shows that Heaven, which governs all things on earth, was regarded with the same respect as the emperors who ruled over the people.

Agriculture was the economic bloodline of ancient China. In a time when there were no fertilisers and modern equipment, successful harvests were solely dependent on weather conditions. Thus, the emperors of China attached great importance to making sacrifices to Heaven for better harvests.

The Chinese even invented the lunar calendar which emphasised the periods for sowing, plowing and harvesting in a year.

This particular association of time and agriculture is also shown in the construction of Tiantan. For instance, the central four pillars in the Qinian Dian (Hall of Prayer for Good Harvests) represent the four seasons. The next 12 pillars around them represent the 12 months of a year. The outer 12 pillars represent the 12 *shichen* (there are 2 hours in 1 *shichen*) of a day. The circumference of the ceiling is 30 *zhang* (a unit of length which equals 3.3 metres) and represents the 30 days of a month.

The wall surrounding Qinian Dian is called Hui Yin Bi (Echo Wall). In the past when there were fewer visitors and less noise, it was possible for people to listen to the whispers along the wall.

Tiantan, a UNESCO World Heritage site, was described by the World Heritage Committee as "a dignified complex of fine cult buildings set in gardens and surrounded by historic pine woods … it symbolises the relationship between earth and heaven—the human world and God's world—which stands at the heart of Chinese cosmogony, and also the special role played by the emperors within that relationship."

LOCATION:
Yongdingmen Dajie, Chongwen District.

TIME-HONOURED BRANDS

Unlike the state-owned stores that were established after 1949, time-honoured brands of Beijing were family businesses and they had their unique way of doing business.

As family enterprises, the owners were keen in promoting short-term and long-term interests. Apart from earning a living from their business ventures, they also wanted their stores to continue to be profitable after their descendants took over their businesses.

Competition was always fierce. Doing business in the capital was even more difficult. It was very difficult to sustain good business over a long period of time when there were no advertisements in the mass media. But these time-honoured brands were able to gain a good reputation for the quality products and good services that had become synonymous with their brand names during their early years.

Tongrentang at Dazhalan Street.

One of the many time-honoured brands found at Dazhalan.

Visitors to Beijing can still see the stores of some time-honoured brands at Liulichang, Dazhalan or Wangfujing. Many of the shops' inscribed boards were executed by famous literary figures of the Qing Dynasty. Some were even inscribed by emperors.

The consumption power of Beijing was definitely the strongest in China. Only in Beijing can people find so many time-honoured brands. And only in Beijing can these stores find so many well-known personalities to endorse their products.

The popular TV series *Dazhaimen* (*Big Courtyard Mansion*) is actually about the history of Tongrentang Chinese Medicine Store. It is said that the playwright and director of the TV series is a descendant of the founder of Tongrentang.

Tongrentang, Huairentang and Heniantang are all Chinese medicine stores. Of the three, the oldest is Heniantang, which was founded in 1525—200 years before Tongrentang.

Back then, a typical well-dressed man had to wear a Majuyuan hat (a hat bought from Majuyuan Hat Store) and a pair of Neiliansheng shoes. His clothes had to be made with cloth from "the eight *Xiangs*" (eight famous fabric stores of the time). Finally, a well-dressed man had to have money in his pocket.

Only the wealthy were dressed in that style. The poor could not afford these luxuries. But Neiliansheng Shoe Store also sells comfortable and inexpensive shoes for the common people.

The eight Xiangs mentioned above refer to the eight fabric stores of the time. They all had the Chinese character '*Xiang*' (meaning 'lucky') in their names. These eight fabric stores all belonged to a particular Meng family of Shandong Province. When the founder of the stores died, these stores were divided among his sons. These stores were financially independent, and they would help one another in times of crisis.

Among the time-honoured brands there are also many restaurants and food stores such as Quanjude (famous for its Peking roast duck), Liubiju (famous for its pickles) and Tongheju Restaurant.

One of the oldest restaurants was called Liuquanju (Willow and Spring Restaurant) for there was a large willow tree and a well in its yard. According to the book *Anecdotes of Beijing* by Xia Renhu, Liuquanju had a history of several hundred years.

Many of the restaurants were courtyard compounds located in small lanes. Guangheju was such a restaurant. Located in Caishikou, the restaurant was famous for its Shandong cuisine.

The façade of this time-honoured shop easily evokes fond memories of the good old days.

TSINGHUA UNIVERSITY

The east gate of Tsinghua University was built with funding from the Tsinghua Class of 1991.

Tsinghua University is one of the two famous universities in China (the other one is Peking University). Tsinghua University was founded by the Americans in 1908. It was funded by the reparations China paid to the United States under the Boxer Protocol.

Tsinghua University is located not far from Yiheyuan (the Summer Palace) and Yuanmingyuan (the old summer palace). The campus of Tsinghua University was originally the private garden of a former official.

Students in Tsinghua at that time had to study for eight years before getting their degree. After graduation, they went to the United States for further studies. The university was different from other universities in China. The principal of the university was appointed by the Ministry of Foreign Affairs instead of the Ministry of Education. Students came from almost every province of China and they all spoke different dialects.

At that time English was used as a medium of teaching and communication by teachers and students in the campus. The students learned American songs and American history. From this, one could see how americanised Tsinghua University was back then. Many graduates of Tsinghua University joined the university as professors after returning from the United States.

New buildings add a touch of modernity to the century-old campus of Tsinghua University.

LOCATION:
Haidian District.

WANGFUJING

Today, Wangfujing usually refers to Wangfujing Avenue. The stretch measures 1.5 kilometres—stretching from Chang'an Avenue in the south to the National Art Museum of China in the north. It is the most popular commercial district in Beijing.

During the periods of Liao and Jin, Wangfujing was merely a small village. Its population escalated after the Yuan Dynasty and it was known as Dingzi Street at that time. During the Ming Dynasty, Wangfujing saw the development of 10 princes' mansions, and it was renamed Shiwangfu Street (Ten Princes' Mansions Street). In the Qing Dynasty, the 'Ten' was taken out and it was called Wangfu Street (Princes' Mansions Street) or Wangfu Avenue (Princes' Mansions Avenue).

In 1915, the then Administration of the Northern Warlords (1912–1927) divided Wangfujing Avenue into three sections. The northern section was called Wangfu Avenue, the middle section was called Bamiancao and the southern section was called Wangfujing Avenue due to the existence of a well (*jing* means 'well' in Chinese).

Back during the Ming Dynasty, vendors had already set up stalls selling silk hats at Wangfujing. By the time of the Qing Dynasty, Wangfujing had become a market place concentrated with shops. With the establishment of Dong'an Market in 1903, Wangfujing became increasingly prosperous. Particularly, the section called Bamiancao—known for its lantern markets—found itself constantly thronged with shoppers. This, in particular, stimulated the commercial growth at Wangfujing.

During the period of the Republic of China, Wangfujing started to experience the first wave of westernisation. Foreign businessmen began to set up shops at Wangfuqing. When Yuan Shikai proclaimed himself as emperor, he renamed Wangfujing as Morrison Avenue as a token of gratitude to a British journalist called George Morrison, who had assisted Yuan in his quest to restore the old imperial system.

During that period, most of the privileged people with power or wealth lived in the east of Beijing. Hence, the many expensive products sold in Wangfujing. Some of the renowned shops

LOCATION:
Wangfujing Dajie, Dongcheng District.
You can get there by subway, getting off at Wangfujing station.

included Wangfujing Department Store, Xushunchang Tailor Shop, Hengdeli Watch Shop, Daming Optician, Tongshenghe Shoe Shop, Shengxifu Hat Shop and Dongxinglou Restaurant. There used to be a theatre called Pheonix Hall as well. It staged performances by great crosstalk artistes such as Hou Baolin and Ma Sanli.

With the founding of the People's Republic of China in 1949, a massive government-led initiative to renovate Wangfujing was launched. Some large-scale business facilities were constructed, with Dong'an Market and Dong'an Department Store forming its backbone.

In recent years, Wangfujing has experienced rapid development and it receives over one million visitors daily. Visitors can find almost everything they need at Wangfujing. The daily trading volume at Wangfujing is tremendous—ranging from clothing to handicrafts, daily necessities to jewels—attracting customers from all walks of life.

DISCOVER BEIJING 153

Dong Fang Xin Tian Di—one of the largest shopping complexes along Wangfujing.

154 DISCOVER BEIJING

DISCOVER BEIJING

The open-air market along the sidewalk of Wangfujing Avenue.

YIHEYUAN

Yiheyuan is probably the best imperial garden in Beijing. It boasts famous scenic spots like Kunming Lake, Shiqikong (Seventeen-Arch) Bridge, Chang Lang (Long Corridor) and Changshou (Longevity) Hill. It would easily take a whole day to explore Yiheyuan.

In 1744, when the construction of Yuanmingyuan (the old Summer Palace) was almost complete, Emperor Qianlong wrote an article recording the whole process. He bragged about the size and beauty of Yuanmingyuan and boasted that it was the best imperial garden ever.

Yiheyuan was primarily built to celebrate the 60th birthday of Emperor Qianlong's mother in 1751. Qianlong ordered a temple built on Weng Hill and he changed the name of the hill to Wanshoushan (Longevity Hill). Along the south side of the hill, pavilions, corridors and palaces were gradually built.

The maintenance of Yiheyuan and other gardens required more and more water. Water for the lakes was mainly diverted from the spring of Yuquanshan Hill (Jade Spring Hill). At the time, water was also needed for the Grand Canal and, fearful that the imperial gardens would run out of water, Emperor Qianlong decided to look for a new source of water for the gardens. He then connected Kunming Lake and the lakes in the old Summer Palace, Yuanmingyuan. Thus Yiheyuan started to take shape.

After Yuanmingyuan was destroyed by the foreign legions following the Boxer Rebellion, the Empress Dowager was determined to build a new summer palace on the grounds of Yiheyuan. At that time, the Boxer Rebellion and wars with Western nations had left China destitute and in disorder. The empress used the money intended for China's navy on the building and restoration of the summer palace at Yiheyuan.

To do so, a so-called naval academy was built inside Yiheyuan. In 1886, the Chinese navy started to practise in Kunming Lake. On 15th December a ceremony was held in the naval academy. The renovation of Yiheyuan started the same day.

Empress Dowager Cixi had hoped to restore Yiheyuan to its original size. Due to limited funds, the plan was abandoned. Only the southern side of Wanshou Hill, West Causeway and the island inside Kunming Lake was renovated. Walls were built

The Ziqidonglai Court at Yiheyuan.

DISCOVER BEIJING   157

A romantic aura surrounds Yiheyuan at dusk.

DISCOVER BEIJING 159

round Kunming Lake. The naval academy was not included in Yiheyuan.

After the renovation, Yiheyuan occupied an area of 290 acres, a little smaller than its original size. The renovation work was completed in 1894, with 97 buildings rebuilt or renovated.

In 1889, two steamers bought from Germany were stationed in Kunming Lake. They were named *Xiangyun* (flying clouds) and *Xiangfeng* (flying phoenix). Electrical lights from Germany were also installed in Yiheyuan.

Ironically, Cixi had actually spent more money on Yiheyuan than Qianlong did. After the renovation work was finished, Cixi spent most of her time in Yiheyuan. She would usually go there in January and would not return to the Forbidden City until November.

Cixi had looked forward to a big celebration for her 60th birthday in 1894. Preparation actually started two years before it. But China lost her navy in a war against Japan just before Cixi's birthday celebration. Cixi thus reluctantly cancelled the celebration in Yiheyuan. But it seemed that she did not care about China's loss at all for she fell in love with Peking opera the next year and was an ardent fan for the next 13 years—having it staged regularly in Yiheyuan.

LOCATION:
Yiheyuan Lu, Haidian District.

YONGHEGONG TEMPLE

The halls at Yonghegong Temple are rich in Tibetan Buddhism elements.

Yonghegong Temple was originally the mansion of Emperor Yongzheng of the Qing Dynasty when he was a prince. After he ascended the throne in 1723 and moved into the Forbidden City, his mansion was converted into a temple for Tibetan Buddhism.

When Tibetan monks arrived in Beijing, they would usually stay in Yonghegong Temple. Inside Yonghegong Temple was the world's largest wooden statue of Maitreya (the future Buddha). It was 18 metres tall and carved from a single piece of white sandalwood. It was a gift from the 7th Dalai Lama (ruler and highest priest in Tibet) to Emperor Qianlong for his help in suppressing a rebellion in Tibet. This expensive white sandalwood block was purchased by the Dalai Lama from Nepal and took three years to be transported to Beijing.

LOCATION:
Yonghegong Dajie, Dongcheng District.
You can get there by subway, getting off at Yonghegong station.

Yonghegong Temple is also famous for its beautiful scenery in winter when it snows. It is a perfect balance of colours to see the red walls and yellow tiles against the white snow.

The famous 18-metre statue of Maitreya, carved from a single piece of white sandalwood.

YUANDADU (Yuan Capital Relics Park)

In 1368, when the Mongolians were driven out of China, Yuandadu—capital of the Yuan Dynasty—was totally destroyed. The only thing left was part of its city walls. Yuandadu means "the city of the Khan" in Mongolian. It was located on the side of Jinkou River. On its ruins, the new capital city of Beijing was built.

The Mongolians had only ruled China for about 100 years before they were driven back to Mongolia. In the following Ming Dynasty, buildings left behind by the Mongolians were demolished. For some years it seemed that the city of Yuandadu had been totally forgotten.

The Italian traveller Marco Polo once stayed in the city of Yuandadu. When he arrived there, Marco Polo was warmly received by Kublai Khan. Kublai Khan was described as a good-looking man of medium build with bright eyes and a straight nose. Marco Polo noted that there were many foreign visitors in the capital. They were soldiers, merchants, travellers, diplomats and missionaries who had either come by sea or via the Silk Road. In the suburbs, there were guesthouses for foreign merchants. People from the same country usually stayed in the same guesthouse.

Yuandadu was a city that became prosperous because of the Silk Road. The Mongolians had conquered a large area of Europe and Asia and therefore, it was relatively safe to travel in these areas. Marco Polo came to China via the Silk Road. According to him, all the best things in the world were traded in Yuandadu. They included pearls, medicines and spices from India. Almost everything could be purchased there. Thousands of carts packed with loads of silk arrived at the city every day. Many small towns around Yuandadu prospered by producing and supplying consumer goods to Yuandadu.

Yuandadu was built as a square city. Each side was 6 miles long. Clay walls were built round the whole city and the watchtowers were painted white. The streets of the city were laid out in a grid system. Within the grid, shops and houses were built—like a big chessboard. The citizens were polite and gentle and there were no quarrels and fights. No locks were needed because nobody stole anything. Lost things were always returned to the owners.

LOCATION:
Southwest of Beitucheng Huandao, Chaoyang District.

Near Jimenqiao, Haidian District.

Such was Yuandadu, a city that had not only left a good impression on Marco Polo, but certainly also on the residents and travellers who had once witnessed the glory of the capital city of the Yuan Dynasty.

The only reminder of Yuandadu can now be found at the Yuan Capital Relics Park in Beijing.

A stone tablet marking the site of Yuandadu at the Yuan Capital Relics Park.

YUANMINGYUAN (The Old Summer Palace of the Qing Dynasty)

Yuanmingyuan (the old Summer Palace) was the emperor's summer retreat. The complex was a collection of Eastern and Western-style buildings. It was called "the garden of gardens" by the Chinese. The emperor stored many jewellery, antiques and precious books in Yuanmingyuan.

In 1860, the British and French Allied Forces occupied Beijing. After the peace accord was signed, they refused to leave Beijing. Instead, Lord Elgin of the British army ordered his soldiers to ransack Yuanmingyuan. More than 3,500 soldiers went away with precious treasures from Yuanmingyuan before setting fire to it. All that was left of Yuanmingyuan was a piece of scorched ground.

Yuanmingyuan became a symbol of humiliation to China. Beijing has left the ruins untouched even as the whole city is

The grandeur of the old Summer Palace is far beyond the imagination of the artists.

166 DISCOVER BEIJING

The ruins left behind by the British after the rampage.

DISCOVER BEIJING 167

168 DISCOVER BEIJING

DISCOVER BEIJING 169

rapidly modernising. It serves to remind the Chinese people to remain vigilant to possible foreign threats even in peacetime.

Only some stone columns and a pair of stone lions have survived the destruction. The scorched lions were originally placed at the gate of Changchunyuan (Garden of Eternal Spring). Now they are at the gate of Beijing Library at Wenjin Street.

Many scholars have tried to draw a map or a picture of Yuanmingyuan. They all failed since few knew what it actually looked like. In 1990, a drawing was found in the Forbidden Palace Museum. The drawing depicts rivers in Yuanmingyuan. But it also points out the buildings and gardens. It is the closest picture to what Yuanmingyuan looked like.

LOCATION:
28 Qinghua Xilu, Haidian District.

YUNJU TEMPLE

LOCATION:
Baidai Hill, Fangshan District.

The cave where Buddhist scriptures are kept in Yunju Temple.

Yunju Temple was built in the Sui Dynasty. It is located about 70 kilometres from Beijing.

Yunju Temple complex includes the temple, Stone Scripture Hill, Scripture Grotto and the Tang Pagodas. It has five courtyards and six halls. To the east of the temple is Shangfang Hill and to the west, Juma River. On both sides of the temple are side halls and rooms reserved for emperors and monks. After the founding of the People's Republic of China in 1949, the temple was renovated twice. Once famous for its "sea of stone tablets and forest of pagodas", there are now only about 20 stone tablets and 10 pagodas left. Other historical sites include Leiyin Cave and Princess Jinxian Pagoda.

The 450-metre high Stone Scripture Hill is located one kilometre east of the temple. In 1981, two fragments of the bone relics of Buddha were found on the hill, which is also famous for the stone tablets with Buddhist scriptures dating back to the Sui and Tang dynasties. The scriptures were carved from the year 605 by a monk called Jingwan.

Over more than a thousand years, 1,122 scriptures were carved on stone tablets. These tablets are located in nine of the caves in Stone Scripture Hill and in the basement of Yunjusi Temple.

The temple is also home to more than 77,000 wooden boards with Buddhist scripture carvings and books of Buddhist scriptures of the Ming Dynasty. Together, they are known as "Three Scriptures".

ZHONGNANHAI

Zhongnanhai was originally called Taiye Lake (Lake of Sacred Water) and located inside Daning Palace, the summer palace of the Jin Dynasty.

During the Yuan Dynasty, a bridge—the Bridge of Golden Tortoise and Jade Rainbow (Jin Ao Yu Dong Bridge)—was added to it. The bridge divided the lake into Beihai (North Sea) and Zhonghai (Middle Sea). In the Ming Dynasty, the lake was further expanded to include Nanhai (South Sea). A man-made isle called Yingtai Isle was also built in the middle of the lake.

The main building in Zhonghai is the Shuiyunxie Pavilion (Pavilion of Water and Cloud). Inside the pavilion there is a stone tablet with the Chinese characters inscribed by Emperor Qianlong of the Qing Dynasty. The four characters are "Tai Ye Qiu Feng" (Autumn Wind of the Taiye Pool).

Ziguangge Hall (Hall of Purple Light) is located at the side of Zhonghai. It was in this hall that Emperor Tongzhi received foreign ambassadors. The palace is about 50 feet high. It is not as majestic as the other palaces but it is still very charming.

At Zhongnanhai, visitors can see a European-style palace nestled among the trees. Looking out of place among all the Chinese-style palaces, this building was the idea of Empress Dowager Cixi. In 1912, after Yuan Shikai was elected as the interim president of China, he chose this Western-style palace as his office.

In 1949, Beijing was taken over by the People's Liberation Army led by Mao Zedong. Mao lived in Shuangqing Villa at Fragrant Hills for two months while Zhongnanhai was being renovated. At first, Mao was reluctant to live in Zhongnanhai for he did not want to be looked upon as an emperor. He later changed his mind and lived there for the rest of his life.

The scenic view of Zhongnanhai.

CHRONOLOGY OF CHINA'S DYNASTIES

?? B.C. – 1122 B.C. — **The Legends Period**
- The Xia (夏) Dynasty (2205 B.C. – 1766 B.C.)
- The Shang (商) Dynasty (1766 B.C. – 1122 B.C.)

1122 B.C. – 221 B.C. — **The Zhou (周) Dynasty**
- The Western Zhou Dynasty (1122 B.C. – 770 B.C.)
- The Eastern Zhou Dynasty (770 B.C. – 221 B.C.)
- The Spring-Autumn Period (770 B.C. – 476 B.C.)
- The Warring States Period (476 B.C. – 221 B.C.)

221 B.C. – 206 B.C. — **The Qin (秦) Dynasty**

206 B.C. – 220 — **The Han (汉) Dynasty**
- The Western Han (206 B.C. – 9)
- The Eastern Han (25 – 220)
- The Three Kingdoms Period (220 – 264)

256 – 420 — **The Jin (晋) Dynasty**

420 – 589 — **The South-North (南北朝) Dynasty**

589 – 618 — **The Sui (隋) Dynasty**

618 – 907 — **The Tang (唐) Dynasty**

960 – 1279 — **The Song (宋) Dynasty**
- The Northern Song Dynasty (960 – 1127)
- The Southern Song Dynasty (1127 – 1279)

1115 – 1234 — **The Jin (金) Dynasty**

1279 – 1368 — **The Yuan (元) Dynasty**

1368 – 1644 — **The Ming (明) Dynasty**

1644 – 1912 — **The Qing (清) Dynasty**

1912 – 1949 — **The Republic of China**

1949 — **The People's Republic of China**

MAP OF CHINA

MAP OF BEIJING

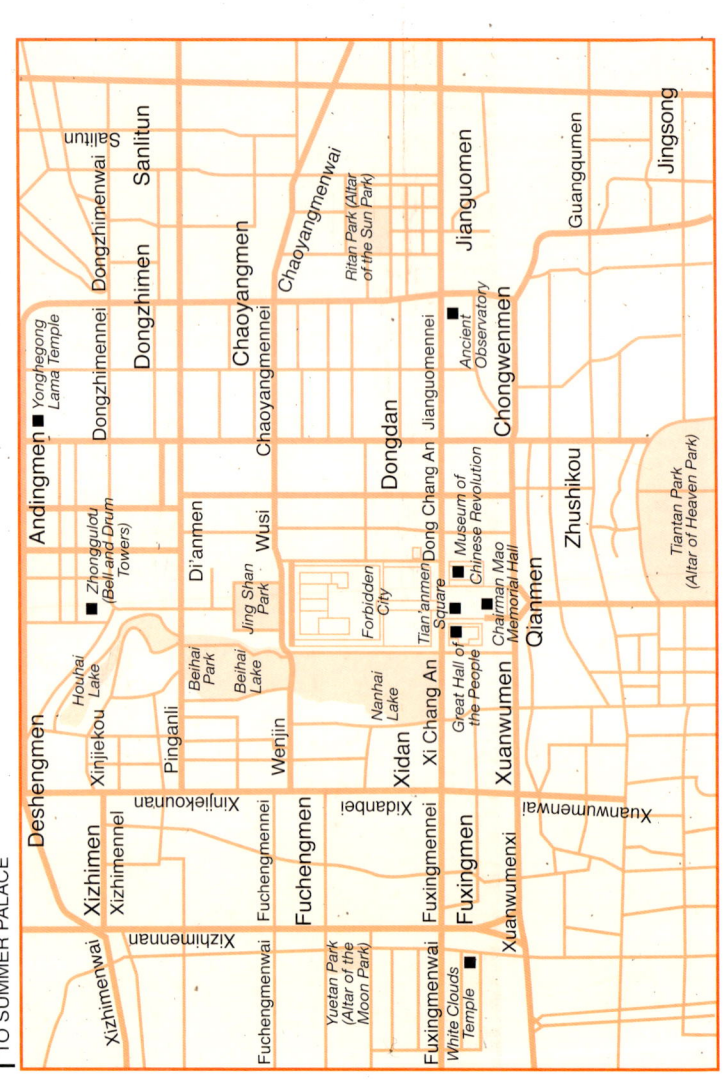